11-21-61

THE FUTURE WON'T WAIT

Harvey A. Everett

THE FUTURE WON'T WAIT

Illustrated by Warren Johnson

FRIENDSHIP PRESS
New York

1961

To my mother and my family

PRINTED IN THE UNITED STATES OF AMERICA
LIBRARY OF CONGRESS CATALOG CARD NUMBER: 61-6041

CONTENTS

This is not
the future's
first burst.
Always it keeps coming
at supersonic speed.

Suddenly in the desert
stands John the Baptist.
"Repent!" he shouts.
"The future—God's future—
the kingdom—is at hand.
It will not wait!"

So Jesus comes.
Are we ready?
Do we welcome him,
love him,
serve him,
see him for what he is?
Or do we go on as before—
hating the Romans,
talking of the price of eggs?

And still the future speeds—
tomorrow starts today.
People move;
Cities grow;
Things change.

In the name of God,
we must do better
than before.
The future will not wait.

WARD L. KAISER

PREFACE

Within the twentieth century man has made tremendous strides scientifically and technologically and is now on the threshold of traveling into outer space. "Change" is the word that characterizes the day in which we live, but "security" and "status quo" seem to be the words that typify the kind of life young people are seeking today.

In the pages ahead, I have tried to present brief sketches of current times and days to come, of the faith required for these times, and of the communities in which this faith must be shared. With these factors as background, I have tried in the fourth chapter of the book to present a consideration of the challenge to the churches presented by these communities. In the concluding chapter are suggestions for ways in which youth may help to extend their church's outreach.

Canada and the United States, along with the rest of the world, are in a definite period of transition. Such a time is always exciting but perilous. Where there are great changes, it is sometimes easy to lose sight of basic values. In many instances, the worst in a new situation may be the easiest to acquire. If changes are not fully understood and evaluated, and if constructive leadership is not given by Christian individuals and institutions, the world of the future may not include the Christian qualities that are so sorely needed.

Change brings with it a sense of urgency to all phases of life. It is my hope that through this book the youth of today will gain that sense of urgency as a member of the Christian church. Young people today face great opportunities as well as awesome responsibilities as we move through "the age of youth."

I am deeply indebted to the American Baptist Home Mission Societies, through whose thoughtfulness the privilege of writing this book was made possible, and for the guidance of Dr. Paul O. Madsen, of those societies, whose personal leadership has inspired so many of the concepts in these pages. I am also sincerely grateful to Beverlee Armstrong, Janice Bailey, and Faith Pomponio for their parts in preparing this book. And to those people who read the manuscript and gave most helpful criticism, I can only say that I hope I have done justice to their suggestions.

HARVEY A. EVERETT

New York City
January, 1961

I

THE AGE OF YOUTH

There are distinctive and unique forces at work in the lives of this and the coming generation of teenagers . . . they are the first teenage generation to have lived their entire lives in the nuclear age . . . they are the first generation of youth in the space era.

DONALD O. NEWBY,
EXECUTIVE SECRETARY,
UNITED CHRISTIAN YOUTH MOVEMENT

Rejoice, O young man, in your youth. . . . But know that for all these things God will bring you into judgment.

ECCLESIASTES 11:9

I

THE AGE OF YOUTH

THE IMPACT OF YOUTH
WHAT'S AHEAD FOR YOUTH?
CHANGING FAMILY PATTERNS
MORE LEISURE, LESS HOME LIFE
THE NEED FOR INDIVIDUALISM

CHAPTER I
The Age of Youth

At no time in history has man been so advanced in his understanding of the universe in which he lives and yet so woefully unable to produce a world of peace, harmony, and good will among men. The twentieth century already has been filled with scientific discoveries and lifesaving achievements beyond the comprehension of even the most optimistic dreamer of an earlier age, but during the same time there have been two world wars and conflicts in Korea, Algeria, the Congo, and countless other areas of tension, as well as the creation of nuclear weapons capable of destroying the world.

In the midst of this age of paradox, the church has an opportunity such as it has never had before. It is the agency through which people may recapture the means and grace of living peaceably. Nothing so strikingly illustrates the necessity for the church of Jesus Christ to succeed in its mission of peace as the threat of instant destruction with which the world is faced.

For instance, picture this scene: Along the east coast of England, sit forty men in front of twenty consoles. "Twenty of the men are United States Air Force officers. Twenty are Royal Air Force officers. In the event of an all-out war, and upon receipt of separate orders from London and Washington, each of the twenty American officers will turn a key on his control console from a position marked 'peace' to a position marked 'war.' Each of the British officers will turn another key in the console. With the turning of the second key in each of the twenty consoles, . . . Thor ballistic missiles will be ready for firing. Each of these . . . intercontinental missiles carries a striking power equivalent to one million tons of high explosive. Each is capable of rising 300 miles into the air and descending on a target 1,700 miles away at a speed of 10,000 miles an hour. Soaring into the skies within minutes of the turning of the keys, these deadly rockets will leave all Europe a blackened, radioactive ruin.

"There will be no second salvo from our launching pads. The men at the keys know that they will be wiped out by the return fire of the enemy within minutes of our own salvo. Not only Europe, but our own continent, too, will be a part of the universal ruin at the end of that apocalyptic day."[1]

This is the background against which our lives are being built. At no time in history has life been so close to extinction and, at the same time, at such an unparalleled point of progress as today. This is indeed an exciting time to be alive. The scope of the rapid changes that have taken place with the twentieth century is staggering when considered according to a time scale devised by Robert E. Wilson, former Chairman of the Board of the Standard Oil Company of Indiana. Compressing the five hundred thousand years of man's development into fifty years, Mr. Wilson worked it out this way:

"On this time scale it took man forty-nine years to get over being a nomad and to settle down in organized communities. . . . About six months ago a few men first learned to write; two weeks ago the first printing press was built. Only

[1] See Notes, page 128.

within the last three or four days have we really found out how to use electricity, around which so much of modern civilization is built!

"And within the very last day have come such amazing things as radio, television, radar, diesel locomotives, rayon, nylon, sulfa drugs, penicillin, bookkeeping machines, electronic computers, high-octane gasoline, color and sound in motion pictures, and hundreds of other things we take for granted. On our condensed time scale, jet planes, dozens of new antibiotics and hormones, and the release of atomic energy all came into the picture this morning."

Today's Christian youth face a future in which they can be a major influence through their faith in determining the course of the world. Much depends upon what they do in these crucial times, for the future won't wait.

THE IMPACT OF YOUTH

In the United States and Canada today, more than one out of every three persons is nineteen years old or under. Youth from fifteen to nineteen will increase by almost 63 per cent between now and 1970, according to a recent study.

Teen-agers are not only a dominant age group, they also are a significant economic force. In the United States alone, they spend around ten billion dollars a year, purchasing items that range from soft drinks to phonograph records to used cars. Numerically and economically, this may be considered the age of youth.

The impact of youth is taking on new significance with the organization of President John F. Kennedy's Peace Corps, to be composed of young American good-will ambassadors who will help people in other nations through such programs as technical assistance and education. Above all, it is hoped, the Peace Corps will enhance understanding between peoples. Thus youth of this age are to play a unique role in a new kind of international diplomacy.

Many Americans face the opportunity of extending the hand of friendship to people right in their own country as well. Although the shores of North America were havens of refuge in the seventeenth, eighteenth, and nineteenth centuries, 1960 saw the beginning of a new era for the United States as it became a place of first asylum for thousands of political refugees from nearby Cuba. These people are the concern of both the Federal Government and of the churches.

What may have always been "foreign" missions for some Protestant North Americans may now become "home" missions as they help to resettle a Cuban refugee family in their midst. People who were once in a mission field beyond our shore now presents a mainland opportunity.

Whether they go overseas or stay close to home, Christian young people have a significant role to play. How well youth is prepared to assume its responsibilities both at home and abroad will determine the progress and course of the world in the next two decades. The role of Christian youth is vital.

WHAT'S AHEAD FOR YOUTH?

What kind of world does youth face in this age that is so close to both life and death? It is a growing, mobile, impersonal world. By the beginning of 1960, there were more than 196 million people in Canada and the United States. It is predicted that by 1975, they will have a total of 249 million people.

Both Canada and the United States have changed from a predominantly rural culture to one that is urban centered. In Canada, by 1975, an estimated six out of every ten persons will live in such communities. The United States is moving even more rapidly into this position, so that by 1975, as today's teen-agers become tomorrow's parents, eight out of every ten people will live in urban areas, that is, areas with populations of more than ten thousand.

In this decade of choices, 1960 to 1970, the average person will move at least twice. People between the ages of eighteen and thirty-five, many of whom have young families, will move on the average of once every three years. Just when a family becomes settled in the neighborhood, school, and church, the husband is transferred somewhere else. These population movements do not produce the close friendships and lasting relations that children and adults require for their finest personal development.

Today life is most impersonal. Though more people actually come in contact with one another than in any other age, few really know one another intimately or genuinely care about one another. Think, for instance, of the familiar greeting, "How are you?" asked automatically, anticipating the automatic reply, "Fine, thank you." Too seldom is the questioner really concerned about the welfare of those whom he greets. He moves too quickly among too many people to be able to share very intimately with any of them.

Life is less home centered than it used to be. For many

people, especially teen-age members of a family, home has become little more than a dormitory, a dining room, and a place in which to change clothes before going elsewhere. This is true despite "togetherness" efforts and such devices as television that would presumably knit families closer together.

CHANGING FAMILY PATTERNS

Family life is being threatened more and more by disruptive forces that frequently result in divorce, alcoholism, and children born out of wedlock. Divorce is one of the most obvious consequences of the destructive elements at work in the home. In Canada there are approximately four divorces for every hundred marriages, or six thousand a year, while in the United States one out of every four and a half marriages ends in divorce. The 800,000 persons who are annually divorced in the United States approximate the present population of such cities as Cleveland, Milwaukee, St. Louis, Washington, D. C., or San Francisco.

In Canada one out of every one hundred residents is an alcoholic or problem drinker, while in the United States 4½ per cent of the population, forming a group of people approximately the size of New York City, fall into this category. Is it not ironic that there are fund drives to eradicate cancer and heart disease and to support mental health programs while alcoholics, who are also sick people, often are scorned and misunderstood by the average citizen? One encouraging sign of the church's recognition of the problem of alcoholism is that the Department of Social Relations of the Canadian Council of Churches has been promoting clergy workshops on alcoholism in association with the Alcoholism Research Foundation.

Children born out of wedlock are another indication of the threats on all sides to the familiar concept of the family and home. Speaking at the annual forum of the National Council of Social Welfare in 1959, Mrs. Katherine Brownell Oettinger, Chief of the Federal Children's Bureau, made public some startling statistics:

"In 1957 . . . 81,000 children were born out of wedlock [in the United States] to teen-age mothers, an increase of 5.2 per cent . . . from . . . 1956. [In Canada some 6,262 babies were born out of wedlock to teen-age mothers in 1957.]

"By 1962, if the rate of births outside of wedlock remains the same, between 110,000 and 120,000 babies will be born out of wedlock to teen-age girls."[2]

This means that 2½ per cent of all children born in the United States in 1962 will have unwed teen-age mothers. Such children often have as parents young people who themselves are products of broken homes or homes in which one or both of the unwed teen-age parents suffered from lack of parental care and guidance. Thus the problems of one generation are handed on to the next.

Family life is undergoing changes that would have been undreamed of during the first quarter of the twentieth century. By the time today's youth are parents of five and ten-year-olds, two out of every three married women will be employed outside the home. More and more children will be reared primarily by other than their own parents. While some children will receive individual care in their own homes during their mother's working hours, many will be cared for in day nurseries and kindergartens with other children of their own age.

The individual American formerly prided himself on being to a large extent self-sufficient and independent. Today he calls on others to assume even the raising of his children. Working parents are forcing their children to sacrifice the privilege of being reared by their own mothers and fathers while the latter are busy earning the money necessary to pay for their children's care and to buy the material possessions they feel they must have. In his book, *The Affluent Society*, John Kenneth Galbraith points out that in this day of spiraling income there is an accent on things; 480 items are considered essential as against 85 listed in 1880.

The growing importance of the acquisition of material things is threatening to outrank even the personal care of children by their parents. Aware of the challenge of this situation, some churches are already providing nursery and kindergarten facilities; yet, they are also asking whether this is an adequate answer.

MORE LEISURE, LESS HOME LIFE

More leisure time than ever before is predicted for the near future as the prospect of a thirty-hour work week looms on the horizon. Changing work patterns, mechanization, and automation have created a situation in which less time is now required to produce goods for sale and distribution. As a result, and under the pressure of labor unions to keep a high level of employment, a four-day work week is likely to become reality.

What will happen then during the three-day week end that this will make possible? The average family will have more time to spend at home in the future, yet it probably will spend more time away from home. For one thing, people will travel more. This will include traveling for pleasure as well as the increased number of hours spent each day by commuters who will live greater distances from their work. Europe is only seven hours away by jet today, and it takes only five hours to fly from New York to Los Angeles. In the United States by 1975, there are expected to be more than 100 million automobiles on the road, operated mainly during the three-day week end.

In order to begin to handle this number of cars, the United States should complete its federal highway program at about the same time most of today's youth are being married. This highway program alone, by taking over present residential areas, will displace one out of every ten people, according to current estimates.

America has been characterized as a nation on wheels, going somewhere constantly. Some people go just for the sake of being on the move, to escape the loneliness of the urban culture in which they live. As a result, they almost never use their leisure for reflection. For youth and adults alike, it might be well to recall that man cannot see himself reflected in running water but only in still water, and that spiritual realities do not shriek or shout out over man's clatter. God comes to us in the stillness, and he speaks to us in our silences.

THE NEED FOR INDIVIDUALISM

Life in this hectic century must be brought into focus, and this can best be achieved by those who are willing to assume individual responsibility. In a period when many people are being

molded into the image of the corporation man, there is a very real need for people who will act as individuals, who have the strength of character to withstand the temptation to conform to the average. American culture today is producing persons who are more concerned about what others think and say about their actions than they are about their own evaluation of what they personally feel, think, and do as individuals. Before they take a stand today, they check to see where others are standing, so they can go along with the crowd. No one likes to be out of step.

A young person has a great opportunity in these changing times to become a real influence for good, to become a real person, to be a leader as his faith guides him in a world that is so wrapped in "things" and so strangled by what "others" think and do that it is rapidly losing its ability to produce individuals with their own inner motivations.

In such a world, what are the driving forces that make a difference in life? What are you really living for? The answer to these questions could be to bring man to a right relationship with God and his neighbors and to restore dignity and worth to the individual. The church today is one of the few institutions that still place the individual first, that realizes that a proper understanding of the needs of the individual man is the beginning of the process of achieving right relationships among people. In the church the individual should be able to discover himself to be a child of God, who has real significance, and who is able to find acceptance and meaningful relationships with others, who also know themselves to be children of God.

II

FAITH FOR CHANGING TIMES

There is a new urgency for us to know more clearly the meaning of our faith and how it is related to the life and death decisions of our generation in this nuclear-space age.

MORAL AND THEOLOGICAL BASES
FOR CHRISTIAN ACTION
IN INTERNATIONAL AFFAIRS

The apostles said to the Lord,
"Increase our faith!"

LUKE 17:5

II

FAITH FOR CHANGING TIMES

OUT OF STEP WITH THE TIMES
REVIVAL OR DECLINE?
CONVENIENCE OF THE COWS
NEW NEEDS, NEW APPROACHES
LARGE GROUPS WERE ONCE POPULAR
LOST IN A CROWD
SOMEONE TO LISTEN
COUNTERING MASS CULTURE

CHAPTER II
Faith for Changing Times

Like the man who stopped halfway up the steps of a famous Chicago museum and, with hands on hips, arrogantly called out to a friend, "What's in there? Anything worth *my* time?", many a potential churchgoer hesitates on the steps of the church to ask, "What's in there? Anything worth my time?"

The inquirer on the threshold of the church might receive a variety of negative answers from people who have not found the church to be the church of the living God. From those who are committed Christians, he might hear a variety of positive answers. One of these might tell him, "In the church I have found life and meaning for daily living in a world that is close to extinction." Another might reply, "I've found purpose and reason for continuing at difficult times in my personal life." Still another might say, "In the church I've found what it means to be accepted and welcomed, no matter what my class, my income, or my race might be."

Every Christian might look critically, yet lovingly, at the church and ask himself, "What's in there? Anything worth my time?" Upon the depth and content of his answer will be determined his effectiveness in communicating what the church is and can be for those who have not yet found it relevant.

To all people—those facing life in its extremities, such as the forty airmen at the control consoles, as well as those experiencing life in its easier moments—the church has a message of hope, of meaningful direction, of concern for the whole man.

In order for the church to implement its message, the emphasis must be on the work of the church, not on "church work"—all the functions that must be performed to keep the church going as an organization. Such functions are necessary and important, but only because they make possible the real work of the church, which is the reconciliation of man to his neighbor and to God.

The church must meet man not solely at the altar, but also at the work bench; not only at prayer meetings, but also at labor-management conference tables; not only in new social halls, but also in teeming slums. The church and its members must be on the frontiers of man's existence, for God is there waiting for his people to work for the reconciliation of neighbor with neighbor and nation with nation. A new generation has the opportunity to lead the church to live out its true purpose, that of doing Christ's work in the world.

OUT OF STEP WITH THE TIMES

The critics of the church are having a field day with the church's application of yesterday's answers to today's needs. This is not to say that Jesus Christ is out of date. It is to say that in many cases the church in its interpretation and presentation of the gospel and in its modes of worship is failing to speak God's message to today's life. In many instances, the language it uses is not relevant for this day. The church continues to speak to problems that are no longer vital and to answer questions that are no longer being asked. Young people must assist the church to develop a message that is pertinent, that speaks to the problems of war and peace, the need for adequate food for all God's children, the formulation of moral standards for this day, and the sacredness of the individual in an age in which he is being depersonalized.

REVIVAL OR DECLINE?

Although statisticians may point to increasing membership rolls in all religious bodies as indication of a religious revival, this does not necessarily indicate a revival of Christianity. There also exists the inescapable fact that Christianity is not holding its own in the population rise in the United States, and this trend could mean that in the future Christians may be in the minority. The decline of Christianity is possible even though there are many churches and even though, in the United States, six out of every ten persons are members of a religious body.

In 1958, there were 109 million persons on the rolls of all United States religious bodies, but at least 21.8 million persons, or 20 per cent, were nonresident members who were not actively aligned with the church in which they held membership. This left 87.2 million people located near enough to the church of

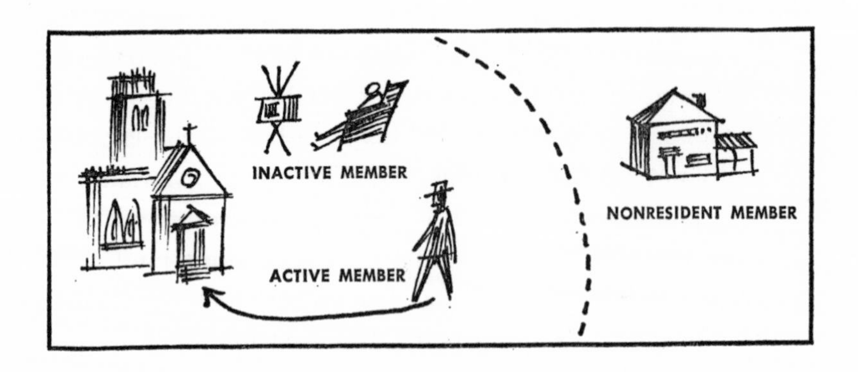

their membership to participate in its program. Of this number, at least 19.2 million were inactive, which left 68 million out of an estimated 173 million people, or 39 per cent of the United States' population active in church or synagogue.[3]

A similar situation prevails in Canada, where 96 per cent of the 17 million residents claim membership in some religious body. Active, dependable adherents of all faiths represent a much lower figure, however.

At the biennial meeting of the Canadian Council of Churches at Saint Catharines, Ontario, in November, 1960, the General Secretary, the Rev. W. J. Gallagher, said:

"In Canada, it might appear that the Churches are doing well. Church membership is increasing, offerings are increasing, new congregations are being organized and new Church buildings are arising—the Church extension programmes are quite remarkable. Church leadership is good, the ministry exhibits high qualities of ability and service, lay movements in the Churches are vigorous and promising, the programmes of evangelism and education and social service and missions are extensive. But are these things good enough, and extensive enough? I cannot avoid this question when I recall that our Churches are not producing enough ministers for their needs, and they are not giving a very large proportion of their income to missions, and there are areas of our life and society upon which they seem to have little influence. . . .

"And what about what used to be called the Christianizing of our social order? What about the changing (should I say declining?) moral standards of our people and our society? What about the pre-suppositions and aims and ideals of our education? What about the cutting off of our culture from its Christian roots? I have a very uneasy feeling about all these. The Churches cannot be complacent about the effectiveness of their mission in Canada."[4]

Something has happened to the church. "Never has the church been materially more powerful and spiritually so weak," according to Henry Steele Commanger. In the midst of a new day, the church has not clothed with power the message of Jesus Christ. Once it was said of Christ's followers, "these men . . . have turned the world upside down." One rarely hears that of the church today. Should not the Christian faith be as vital in the twentieth century as it was to Christ's disciples in the first century? If it is not, why not? One clue may be found in knowing the needs of God's people and developing means of meeting those needs. The church in some ways is not geared to today's living.

CONVENIENCE OF THE COWS

The times set for worship and church school classes are indicative of how out of step the church is with today's culture. Most Protestant churches schedule worship at eleven o'clock on Sunday morning and have church school sessions before the service of worship instead of after. Evening worship, when held, usually begins around seven or seven-thirty on Sunday, and the youth group meeting is generally before the evening service instead of after it.

The reason for such timing is that both Canada and the United States were once nations that revolved around the farm. True to the teaching of the Master when he said, "The sabbath

was made for man, not man for the sabbath," rural people attempted to adjust the sabbath and times of services to suit man's needs. Prior to the advent of the automobile and the modern milking machine, eleven o'clock was a practical hour for worship. It allowed the farmer time to do his milking and other morning chores before taking the family to church. As someone jokingly has said, "We worship at the convenience of cows, not men." The fact that the family wanted to come home together helped set youth meetings before the evening service.

But times have changed. Fifty years ago, one out of every three persons lived on farms. Today in the United States, only one out of every eight persons is a farm resident. As the number of farm residents decreased, the number of farms also declined. The total acreage of land used for agriculture changed little, however, for the size of farms increased proportionately. According to the most recent figures available, more than 50 per cent of all Canadians and Americans live in urban areas of ten thousand or more.

Though the number of farm people in rural North America also is decreasing annually, the pattern of Protestant church services still follows the time set primarily for the farmer. The trend has been so much away from agriculture, even in rural areas, that the church needs to examine both the hours of its services and its program.

NEW NEEDS, NEW APPROACHES

The average work week used to be six days, Monday through Saturday; Sunday was the day of rest. Today in North America some people work on Sunday and others work through the night. There is no universal nine-to-five work shift, which means that for some Protestants church services are always held during their working hours.

Many people pass a church five days a week during their lunch hour but are not near one on Sundays. With the prospect that people will increasingly be on the road or staying at a resort over the three-day week end, fewer will be in their home communities on Sunday. The change from rural to urban living, the shift in work patterns, and the projected long week end suggest that perhaps the times of worship, even the day of worship, need expansion or adjustment.

In the future the Protestant might belong to two churches, a week-day church in the community in which he lives or works and a week-end church where he spends his week ends, perhaps in a resort community. The local church could meet a real need by providing, in addition to the traditional Sunday services, one on Thursday or Friday evening or early Friday morning before people leave Friday night for the long week end. The Sunday evening service might come back into prominence as an alternative time at which people could worship on their way home.

Some Protestant churches do encourage week-day worship

such as early morning Communion services, and one church in a community that is practically deserted on the week end holds a Friday evening vesper service. One large denomination at an annual meeting raised the question of whether the conventional hour and day of worship do not need to be reconsidered in light of changing cultural and work patterns. Such changes could be the means of meeting man's need for the changeless message. Merely adjusting the hours of worship will neither enlist nor hold members. Nevertheless such adjustments provide one way of keeping the church in step with changing cultural patterns and thus implementing the real work of the church.

LARGE GROUPS WERE ONCE POPULAR

When interest in religious education developed, the church school came into being. Farm conditions, which set the hour of worship at eleven o'clock, also governed who could attend this new facet of the church's life. The wife and children were not tied down by morning chores, so they were able to leave for church earlier. The family always came home together; this seemed to be an unwritten rule in the family life of the day. Thus, to meet the religious education needs of children, Sunday school was set before worship, at ten o'clock in most instances.

The day of the large church school class was also a product of a rural-farm culture. All week long people worked and lived in small groups. Their nearest neighbors were probably miles away so they were limited to the society of their own family. They developed a desire to be with people in church and other community gatherings. Church suppers at which people from the whole countryside gathered were the result of a need for fellowship as well as a need to raise money. Large Sunday school classes also became opportunities for socializing as well as for religious education. The men often were grouped in one large class, the women in another. Having been with their families most of the week, men and women felt a real need for joining with others in a larger group of Christians at worship and in church school.

LOST IN A CROWD

Today in an urban-centered continent, the people of Canada and the United States are part of a mass culture. No longer do they find themselves isolated as did their forefathers. Their way of life throws them together with thousands of people whom they do not know. Whether they travel by car, subway, bus, or train, they are part of a crowd. Many must travel in large groups every day, for they live in one community and work in another. The average worker is part of such a huge labor force that he only knows those people who are in his immediate vicinity at the factory or office. Even recreation is affected by mass culture; people form audiences of thousands, either in person or via a

television network to observe sports such as soccer, hockey, boxing, baseball, and basketball.

Housing, too, is crowded together either in tall apartment houses and developments or in tract developments of monotonous similarity. Shopping is no longer the intimate activity of bygone days when there was a clerk-customer relationship. The supermarket at the shopping center is almost completely depersonalized. People used to know one another in small communities, but today in urban areas they seldom know their next door neighbor; nor do they seemingly want to. The individual used to be supreme, but today it is the organization that is supreme. The individual is important only as long as he adequately serves the organization.

Instead of wanting to be in one more crowd at church, people seek out small groups in which they can be real individuals and come to know themselves and others. They want to experience a feeling of acceptance that they lack in a crowd. In place of the large adult or older youth class of yesterday, buzz groups and other small, face-to-face discussion of groups are in some ways answering the individual's need to discover himself and make himself heard. Worship services in which comparatively few people participate may be more valuable than a large service in which individuals feel lost in the crowd.

When they do not find the fellowship they seek in the church, people often go elsewhere. Vance Packard's book, *The Status Seekers,* mentions a study that reveals that the average person who frequents a tavern lives within two blocks of the tavern that he patronizes. He is there from fourteen to twenty-four hours a week and spends an average of eighteen dollars during that time. His primary purpose in going to the tavern is not to drink but to talk to and be with people who share interests and needs similar to his.

SOMEONE TO LISTEN

Not many years ago the church served the purpose of fellowship and provided opportunity for good discussion. People have a deep desire to exchange ideas with one another. A morning newspaper once carried an advertisement that read: "Willing to listen for $1.00 an hour." The person who advertised listened attentively to anything his clients wanted to talk about but gave no advice. Within a short time the number of people who sought his services had so increased that the listener doubled his price and hired a staff to help him listen to people talk.

Although the average person does not want merely a sounding board for his thoughts, he does want the opportunity of expressing and exchanging his ideas with others so that he may find fellowship in the world in which he lives. He seeks to share his ideas, discuss the issues of the day, and learn what the church has to say.

The church must face the loneliness that is produced by the growing lack of concern of people for one another. The daily occurrence of the man robbed of his self-respect, lying beside the Jericho Road of our day with the world passing him by, is so familiar that it is dulling man's compassion for God's needy children. The individual members of the church must restore a personal concern for the people around the church's door and thus begin to re-create a sense of oneness and wholeness in each individual's life as he is given recognition as a person of value.

COUNTERING MASS CULTURE

The impersonal culture of today must be met with a warmth and depth of fellowship and concern for the individual that the church can give through its face-to-face groups. Growing industrialization and automation that make it all but impossible for an individual ever to see anything through to completion must be countered with opportunities for creativity within the church through the arts such as music and religious drama. An expression of creativity can also be achieved through emphasis on the individual's witness as he seeks to relate others to the Christian way of life. Creation of firm moral standards must be faced in this day when values of all kinds are disintegrating. This means facing this problem in the church honestly and without fear.

Laymen of all ages must assume real responsibility for the outreach of the church. The vital importance of children and youth in the church has been stressed through programs of education and young people's activities, but young people's resources of talent and leadership often go untapped and their interest in the church is lost. A problem here may be lack of communication between adults and youth.

In developing an adequate witness for today, the church must move toward new policies of leadership and training as they relate to young people. Youth may be used for leadership now and trained for more responsible positions in the future by being given opportunities to participate as junior members of church boards and committees and as apprentice deacons, stewards, elders, and trustees.

Christian young people should look at the manner in which Jesus Christ faced the traditions of the past. He sought to free man from religion's dead weight in order that he might worship and serve God and make his faith a joyous portion of his life. What is the young person's responsibility today? Will he help to develop new methods by which the Christian gospel will speak to the needs of people in the days ahead? Will it be said of today's Christian youth that they "turned the world upside down"? Or will conformity cause them to accept the old ways as those before them too often have done?

Changes in hours of service, the addition of face-to-face groups, the stress on the individual, new programs in the arts, and increased activity for all ages within the church, however, will not replace or compensate for an inadequate personal commitment to God. The church cannot and must not apologize for demanding the surrender and commitment of each individual at the cross of Christ. Such commitment often demands that Christians serve those who, according to their human standards, do not merit their compassion. Yet the Christian's role is to serve not only where life is pleasant but also where it is rough and disheartening. Changes must occur, and there must be a witness of the faith that will win the person standing on the steps saying, "What's in there? Anything worth my time?"

This will happen only if each church and each church member look at the needs of the new day and then prayerfully and joyfully retool their programs and methods to meet them.

The faith these times demand must be more than a faith in faith. It must be a personal, growing faith in God and his will for each individual's life. This faith must be communicated to every person.

III

WHERE DO YOU LIVE?

We are all on the move.
From rural areas to the city, from inner
city to the suburbs and back again, from north
to south and south to north, east to west
and west to east . . . from reservations
to cities and small towns.

"EDGE OF THE EDGE,"
BY THEODORE E. MATSON

". . . where are you staying?" . . . "Come and see."

JOHN 1: 38, 39

III

WHERE DO YOU LIVE?

CHAPTER III
Where Do You Live?

Cities and villages usually develop in relation to basic requirements of people and industry. The major American and Canadian cities of today, such as Toronto, New York, Boston, Montreal, San Francisco, Vancouver, New Orleans, Chicago, Detroit, and Halifax, grew up around the water routes. In the open country areas where there were no major waterways, villages and towns sprang up around the transportation arteries that were developing for the growing nations. At stagecoach stops, railroad stations, trading posts, lumber centers, and major crossroads, towns and villages began. As the nations grew, more and more communities came into being to house the increasing population, and some developed into the major cities of the two nations.

If someone were to ask you, "Where do you live?", you probably would answer by giving the name of your street or the city or town in which your home is located. But if your questioner were to ask you, "What kind of community do you live in?", could you answer accurately? In days gone by "village," "town," or "city" would have been adequate, but today's classifications are far more complex.

No longer is the country just the country, for many rural communities are being absorbed into the metropolitan areas that are spreading out across the face of the North American continent. Even the rural areas are subdivided into farm and nonfarm communities.

THE URBAN COMMUNITIES

Urban communities are here considered as being areas with populations of ten thousand or more people. Before the rate of urbanization reached its present intensity, it used to be possible, merely by going from the downtown district out to the suburbs, to locate where the slums and deteriorating areas of a city were, as well as where the homes of the economically well-off were situated. There seemed to be a direct relationship between the social and economic status of people and the distance of their residence from the oldest areas of the city. The slums and "skid row" usually were near the commercial, downtown area.

Today, because nearly every city is in a state of flux, business districts and residential areas are in various stages of disintegration, or regeneration—often called urban renewal. The city is constantly changing—former residents are moving out, and new people are moving in, making new uses of existing buildings; or whole blocks are falling under the blows of wreckers' hammers. Neighborhoods that once were purely residential are becoming commercial as homes give way to warehouses and small manufacturing plants. On the other hand, former business districts are becoming luxurious residential areas as modern, expensive apartment houses rise on the scene. As land use and function change so inevitably does the complexion of a neighborhood.

Within a city or urban area, there may exist a number of communities such as "the inner city," "a transitional neighborhood," "a suburb," and even the "rural-urban fringe." Let us examine each of these communities in turn.

The Inner City

The inner city usually is a neighborhood in which deteriorating buildings and brand new luxury apartments stand within one another's shadows. The once elegant mansions of decades past are no longer well kept but instead have been converted into offices for doctors, lawyers, and charitable organizations, or, having already served in those capacities, have been further converted into rooming houses as their last use before being demolished to make way for new housing. Apartment houses may be old and rundown, grouped together in huge public or private housing developments, or modern individual towers of air-conditioned luxury.

The people who live in the old housing of the inner city generally are different culturally, economically, and often racially from those who first occupied the buildings. Economically underprivileged newcomers generally settle in the deteriorating buildings of the inner city when they first come to a city. The rents usually are low, and the apartments and rooming houses are open to anyone who can pay the rent.

Where once relatively few people lived, vast numbers are

crowded into a small area. In one inner city neighborhood in New York, four thousand people live in one square block where normally not more than five hundred people should live. The inner city often is synonomous with slum.

The inner city erroneously is called the melting pot, where all races and conditions of men come together. There is little real melting, however, for the residents do not become one. Usually there is only boiling. Life easily breaks down in these tense, crowded, and sometimes subhuman ways of existence.

Few people want to live in the inner city, but many must because they can afford to live nowhere else, or because the color of their skin makes them unwelcome elsewhere. According to the United States Bureau of the Census, one out of every four persons in the United States today lives in substandard housing, much of which is in the inner city, though slums also exist in small towns and villages. Comparable figures for Canada are not available, but informed people feel that one out of every seven Canadians lives in substandard housing today.

The Transitional Neighborhood

If they move progressively up the economic and social ladder, the transitional neighborhood may be the second place to which people move after initially going to the city. The housing available for them usually is old but not quite so rundown as the old inner city dwellings. Industry and business either are beginning to or have already invaded the residential sections of the transitional neighborhood. Many of the residents are "captives" who would like to move but cannot, usually because they cannot afford to.

Clashes may occur in the transitional zone when those who have lived in the area all their lives seek to keep the minorities from invading their neighborhood. Teen-age gang rivalries often burst into violence as fears and prejudices of different ethnic groups get out of hand. Adults, too, sometimes resort to uncivilized tactics to keep "undesirables" out of their community. They fear the newcomers will overrun the area and cause property values to fall. It cannot be said, however, that such will happen. Rumor and fear of the unknown are among the worst enemies of the transitional community. Fear produces confusion, and confusion produces disorganization. A community without a stable group of residents soon slips into decay.

The Suburbs

Beyond the city limits are the suburbs, which are an important segment of the urban picture. They may be described as the stable residential communities, the tract communities, or the bedroom communities. The older suburbs have grown gradually, as the houses were built individually or in small developments. The tract or bedroom communities that cover thousands of acres began to blossom around American and Canadian cities right after World War II.

Who were the people who first moved to the suburbs, and why did they move? Most of them came from the middle class homes that once flourished in what are now the inner city areas. When the exodus to the suburbs first began, the city people who did not move thought those who did were mad to go "such a distance" from the city's center. The new suburbanites moved for a variety of reasons. Some wanted more room than they could find in the city. Others wanted to raise their children in the country. Still others moved because they did not want to live side by side with the racial and lower income groups that gradually were moving into the inner city. The improvement of commuting service by rail and bus made it possible for the husband to travel a considerable distance to and from work with relative ease.

The "baby boom" that began in 1941 and the need and desire of young couples to purchase their own homes resulted in thousands of acres of farm land and open country all around cities being converted into housing sites. Where once there were fields, there soon stood thousands of tract-type houses, containing one or two bedrooms. The latest modern gadgets were included in these houses, but they were usually of the cheapest quality. The basic design of all the houses in each development was alike; only the color of paint on the exterior of the houses was different, and that was repeated on every third house.

John C. Keats, author of *The Crack in the Picture Window*, caustically describes this type of housing:

"For literally nothing down—other than a simple two per cent and a promise to pay, and pay, and pay until the end of your life—you can own a box of your own in one of the fresh-air slums we're building around the edges of America's cities. Even while you read this, whole square miles of identical boxes are spreading like gangrene throughout New England, across the Denver prairie, around Los Angeles, Chicago, Washington, New York, Miami—everywhere. In any one of these new neighborhoods you can be sure all other houses will be precisely like yours, inhabited by people whose age, income, number of children, problems, habits, conversation, dress, possessions and perhaps even blood types are precisely like your own."[5]

This may be an overly pessimistic presentation, yet it is truer about some of today's tract housing developments than some people like to believe.

In the tract communities young couples find themselves associating only with people in their own age group and income bracket. The majority of couples have young children, and there are very few teen-agers. The monotony of being just like everybody else produces all kinds of problems for husbands and wives, for their children, and for the church and community.

Zoning laws may prevent the addition of an extra bedroom as more room is needed for a growing family. As a result, mobility in the one- and two-bedroom communities is high. Some couples stay up to twelve years, but many move after four to eight years. The age of the children, the need for more room, the desire for a new location, or the transfer of the husband, plus the fact that the family income has increased, provide some of the reasons for families in the two-bedroom communities to move to the three- and four-bedroom communities. Other young families take their place, and the cycle is started over again.

The houses in the three- or four-bedroom communities may also be mass produced, but they usually are more expensive than the one- and two-bedroom variety. Again the residents are similar in background, age, and economic status. The average couples in the three- and four-bedroom suburb are in their thirties and forties, and their older children are in their teens.

Another type of suburb is the custom-built community, which usually is located a considerable distance from the city and may be synonymous with prestige and importance. Only a relatively small proportion of the population ever reaches this stage of suburban life, for few people can afford to live in the houses that start at $40,000. Each house is individual in its design and landscaping. Age-wise the custom-built community is well balanced, though there are proportionately fewer young couples than elsewhere in suburbia. Most adults are over thirty-five; and there are from one to five children, many of them in their teens. This type of community is made up primarily of business executives—the men who direct the business and industrial affairs of the nation—and the elite of the entertainment, educational, and social worlds.

The Rural-Urban Fringe

Out in the country, just beyond the suburbs, is the rural-urban fringe. Here small villages used to be set off by themselves. Gradually, as the city spread, the once isolated villages have become part of the city. There are thousands of such communities in the United States and Canada, and as the population explosion continues, there will be more.

As city peoples' desire to live in the country increases, family-size farms are being converted and remodeled, and new homes are being built. The "city" people who move to the rural-urban fringe have their roots culturally and economically in the city so that they find it difficult to adjust to the somewhat "sleepy" atmosphere of their new home. Villages and towns that enjoyed an unruffled way of life for generations do not always react happily to the newcomers and their "city" ways, and it is often difficult for the town fathers to see any value or need to adopt their ideas. Newcomers, on the other hand, want more modern approaches to such aspects of civic life as education, recreation, shopping, and health facilities, and police and fire protection services.

THE SMALL TOWNS AND VILLAGES

Outside the metropolitan area are the small towns and villages that are still separate municipal entities. Some are centers of agricultural activities; others are mining, lumbering, fishing, resort, and even college and military communities. In the United States today three and a half out of every ten persons live in such communities, while in Canada four out of every ten people live in communities of less than ten thousand inhabitants.

There are many ways to describe villages. Originally their structure revolved around the country store, the church, and the one- or two-room schoolhouse. Today, with the consolidated school program, many of the original schools are either vacant or have been converted into living quarters.

Some village communities are dwindling in population. Declining population is the result of changes in employment and the technological advances in agriculture that make it possible for fewer farmers than ever before to produce greater quantities of food and fiber than their predecessors. For the declining small communities, the church and the small country store often remain the center of the area.

On the other hand, some village communities are growing. The decentralization of businesses and the increased use of trucks for transporting goods have enabled manufacturers to locate plants in rural areas, which have consequently taken on new life. In still other instances, the growing desire of people to have a second home in the country has caused rural areas within driving distance of the larger cities to have part-time residents in their midst. The vast highway system is making this more practical.

These areas are not to be dismissed lightly in a growing urban culture. Many of the fine characteristics ascribed to rural society are desperately needed in urban life. The warm friendship, the close fellowship, and the real concern of old friends for one another that are often associated with rural areas should be rekindled in the large, impersonal, sprawling cities. The rural resident's civic pride is a characteristic that would be a stabilizing factor if it could be developed in urban transitional areas.

The rural areas, however, are not without their disadvantages and problems. Declining employment opportunities have forced thousands of young people to move elsewhere, often to cities, to find work. The sometimes difficult problems that face the newcomer who settles in a rural community must not be ignored, for, in some instances, one remains an outsider until he has lived in a village for a number of years.

Changing population means that the people of many of the

rural communities will have to adjust their school system and church organizations so that these two forces may remain strong and effective. Those who try to help a community retool for increasing opportunities and new residents may have to counter the objections of some long-time residents of the community who balk at any proposed changes.

THE TRAILER VILLAGE

The trailer has come a long way since it was first used for vacations only. Back in the days before World War II, the trailer was a small unit that could be hitched to the rear of an automobile and pulled along with relative ease. It had little in the way of conveniences, but it was sufficiently well equipped to enable a family to use it for a camping holiday. During the war, servicemen bought up trailers by the thousands and used them as temporary housing for their families, whom they wanted to keep near them for as long as possible before they had to leave for overseas duty.

As the trailers became "home" for G.I. couples, they were improved in size, quality, and conveniences. Today they are longer, wider, and much like permanent houses. Some have as

many as three bedrooms and even two levels. They are furnished with the latest equipment and labor-saving devices. They are far too big to be pulled behind the family car and must now be hauled by special pick-up trucks.

Called mobile homes, they are no longer used primarily by transients but actually are permanent homes for many people. Surrounding American cities today are attractive modern trailer villages. In Florida, Arizona, and California, mobile homes serve as residences for senior citizens as well as for young families with one or two children.

ARMED FORCES COMMUNITIES

Like the trailer villages, the armed forces communities are products of changing times. With the universal military training program of the United States, many young men spend two to four years in the service of their country. America's military personnel largely is married, so that the armed forces community today encompasses whole families. Many live in the housing that increasingly is being provided on military bases for servicemen and their dependents, but a great many airmen, soldiers, sailors, and marines prefer to live in communities near their bases. Although the rate of mobility is high for the civilian, the military man and his dependents provide an even more dramatic example of America on the move. Some of the problems facing much-on-the-move service families are loneliness; brief assignments; poor base-community relationships in some areas; inadequate pay and poor financial arrangements for some; illness, especially of mothers with small children; inadequate housing at reasonable rents; and child care for working mothers.

While there is no draft program for the armed forces in Canada, there are substantial numbers of persons in the services. In some instances they also have a community life with their families, similar to that in the United States.

WHAT DOES IT ALL MEAN?

As you have read through the descriptions of the various communities, what has it meant to you as a young person?

First, it should tell you something of the divisions of urban and rural areas about which you may not have been aware.

Second, it is a preview of some of the kinds of communities in which you will live, whether you marry or remain single.

Third, it gives you some background for the discovery of the new kinds of churches that are needed for the communities of today and tomorrow.

"Where do you live?" Though your community may be a mixture of the neighborhoods described, most likely you can now identify with some accuracy the type of community in which you and your family live. Your answer to "Where do you live?" is very important, but far more vital is your answer to "What concern do you have for the community and its spiritual welfare?" Each community has differences that distinguish it from any other. These differences demand special kinds of churches, both in terms of buildings and programs. You and your friends will help to make some of the decisions that will answer the question, "What concern do you have for the community and its spiritual welfare?"

IV

CHURCHES FOR TODAY AND TOMORROW

A realistic look at contemporary America has . . . to be taken by the churches if they are to serve its burgeoning population.

MERYL H. RUOSS, CHAIRMAN,
DIVISION OF CHURCH STRATEGY
AND DEVELOPMENT,
BOARD OF NATIONAL MISSIONS,
UNITED PRESBYTERIAN CHURCH
IN THE U.S.A.

To him be glory in the church and in Christ Jesus to all generations, for ever and ever.

EPHESIANS 3:21

IV

CHURCHES FOR TODAY AND TOMORROW

THE DOWNTOWN CHURCH
THE TRANSITIONAL CHURCH
THE APARTMENT CHURCH
THE SUBURBAN CHURCH
THE CHURCH IN THE CUSTOM-BUILT SUBURBS
THE RURAL-URBAN FRINGE CHURCH
THE VILLAGE CHURCH
CHURCHES FOR MILITARY COMMUNITIES
THE COLLEGE OR UNIVERSITY CHURCH
THE TRAILER CHAPEL
OTHER FACETS OF CHURCH EXTENSION
YOUTH'S RESPONSIBILITY

CHAPTER IV
Churches for Today and Tomorrow

If current urban redevelopment and renewal plans for Detroit are carried out in the next ten to fifteen years, 187 Protestant churches will be demolished, according to the Rev. Richard Cummings of Detroit. Only the members of a few of the 187 churches realize that their buildings stand in the path of the city's rehabilitation programs. This is not a unique situation; rather it is an example of what faces many churches in the United States and Canada as cities are rebuilt in this changing age. The future of many North American neighborhoods and communities already has been or will be determined by city and regional planning commissions. Today the community often alters the church and its program. In the case of older areas in the great major cities such as Detroit, a community's future often determines whether the church building will remain or be destroyed.

When today's senior citizens were teen-agers, the church was the center of community life, and it often determined the community's stand on certain issues. The church building frequently was used as the gathering place for the discussion of problems facing the town or village. The church's voice was one that carried great weight. Today the church sometimes abandons its leadership role by withdrawing from the community and leaving the political and other matters to politicians or secular organizations. In forsaking its community responsibility, the church may find that its future is decided by those it knows only as "the people down at city hall," whom it does not know. The church that is alive in its community can help to shape not only its own future but also that of its neighborhood and region. If it does not, its future may be determined without its consent by city planners, as some of the 187 churches in Detroit may discover all too late.

It was not long ago that most people lived, worked, shopped, attended church and school, and had their friends all in one community. But, in this day of vast metropolitan areas, that is no longer true. Today one family may be related to as many as six different communities. The husband may work in one community, the wife shop at the large shopping center in another community. In some instances the church that such a family attends may be in another place, and their friends and clubs and other activities may take them still elsewhere. Only in some rural areas is the church the geographical center of the community, and even here it is often not the life center of the community and its residents. Instead the church often must compete with the community's many other activities for a family's time.

Today's young people live in many different kinds of communities, and will move to a number of different types of neighborhoods during their lifetime. This age of new communities and of revitalization of old ones offers wonderful opportunities for the church to extend itself to meet the growing demands of this era.

What is meant by the term church extension? It is often thought of primarily in terms of planting the church in areas on the growing edge of a city where new church buildings and congregations are badly needed. It is necessary, however, to think also in terms of the extension existing churches will be required to make in many types of communities. Whether it be an entirely new congregation and church in one of the suburban rings, or a new concept of its task by an existing church—such as a transitional church in the inner city or a new program for a village church—each is an example of the church extending itself to meet a new age.

Clues to the future may be found in an examination of how some of the churches of today are meeting the challenges of these times.

THE DOWNTOWN CHURCH

"Downtown" usually designates the old area of a city; sometimes today it is called the inner city. Among the downtown churches may be old First Church, so called because it was the first congregation of its denomination to be established in the city. At one time its membership may have been the largest in the entire denomination. It may still be the congregation with the greatest prestige, but in all likelihood its membership is probably declining now as its people move to the various suburban rings surrounding the city.

Even when they move, members at first come back to their old church. Eventually, the distance, the desire of the teen-agers to attend the youth group of the neighborhood church with their school friends, and the need for all the family to be in the same church cause many families to transfer their membership to a suburban church. At this time of transfer, they may change membership from one denomination to another or they may seek a new church home in the same communion.

When the majority of members lived within the church's community, a one- to two-mile radius, there were activities almost every night of the week. Things are different now. The church, once surrounded by one-family houses, is now engulfed by office buildings and even industrial plants. Many of the homes around the church may be substandard.

There may be more people living within the shadow of old First Church now than when it was started. Some people may be socially, racially, or economically different from the original members. Many may be young, single career men and women, new to the city. Still others may be older people who are widowed or retired or whose children have grown and left home. Many among this last group may have returned to the city after living for a number of years in the suburbs or the rural-urban fringe.

Old First Church could be illustrated by many examples in Canada and the United States. A striking example of a downtown church that is adapting its program to the needs of the people in its community is First Baptist Church of Boston. Many changes have come to this historic church that was founded in 1665. It has merged with three other congregations to form its current membership. Its present building was purchased from a former Unitarian church. Like most churches that flourished in the eighteenth century, some of its early support came from the sale and rental of pews. The front pews brought the highest fees, while seats in the balcony and the back rows sold for the lowest prices.

First Baptist Church of Boston is located on Commonwealth Avenue, near the famous Beacon Hill section. As the United States has changed since the days of Washington and

Adams, so has the community of First Baptist Church. Where the brownstone mansions of many of the nation's great men once stood, today rise modern apartment buildings. The mansions that still stand on Commonwealth Avenue and the nearby side streets have nearly all been converted into rooming houses. Senior citizens and young career people share this community with a few wealthy families that remain.

The Rev. Edward L. Gunther, the pastor of First Baptist Church of Boston, has but a short walk from the church to one of the city's slums. Two miles away is the West End Redevelopment Project, where old substandard housing is being demolished and new apartment and office buildings are being erected. Changes that come about with the aging of housing often are accompanied by changes in the kind of people who live in the houses. This has happened to the community around First Baptist.

Many years ago there was an immigration of young Chinese men to Boston. They settled in a district less than a mile and a half from First Baptist that is now known as Chinatown. First Baptist saw a new need in Chinatown and developed a new facet of its missionary work to meet it. Classes in English and Bible were held for the Chinese men. Out of the English classes grew a Chinese Sunday school, which through the years has served many of the Chinese people of Boston. The Chinese church school is still held every Sunday afternoon, but the need for it has almost passed.

As the neighborhood has changed so has the church's program. Religious education for children of all ages was once foremost at First Baptist Church. Today it has been modified considerably, because large numbers of children no longer live in the vicinity of the church. First Baptist Church and the other downtown churches of Boston—Copley Square Methodist Church, Trinity Episcopal Church, and Old South Congregational Church—were at one time largely composed of young families with children. Today their congregations include few young families and many single persons. First Baptist Church seeks to relate the single people into family groups and provide both fellowship and religious training for them.

The pastor is not nearly as busy with formal Sunday services as were his predecessors twenty-five years ago. The church has only one worship service at eleven o'clock with church school classes preceding it at ten o'clock. The evening service was discontinued some years ago because of the small attendance and little interest. On an average Sunday there are between 250 to 400 present in the nine-hundred-seat sanctuary. When there was no minister, just before Pastor Gunther went there in 1957, the church had as few as one hundred present on some Sunday mornings.

Two-thirds of the congregation of First Baptist Church is made up of women. Most of the adults are over the age of fifty, which is common in downtown churches. There are some couples. The younger couples either commute from the suburbs or live in nearby apartments. The older couples usually are those with grown children who have moved back into the city to live in an apartment.

There are no junior or senior high youth groups at First Baptist. There are, however, young adult fellowship groups for college students and those young people who are working. There is also a group of senior citizens who plan and carry out a program of weekday activities. Discussion groups operate throughout the church program. Through them the church seeks to break down the depersonalizing influence of modern city culture. One phase of the pastor's ministry is helping the people become a significant part of the church by assisting them to find personal acceptance and expression in small groups.

When he first wanted to visit the people who lived near the church, Mr. Gunther found that the apartment houses were normally locked to anyone who did not have the name of the person he sought. Therefore, he had to use a new approach to solve a new problem. First, he acquired a reverse telephone directory that listed telephone numbers by street address rather than alphabetically by name. In this way he secured the phone numbers of persons who lived within the vicinity of the church. The senior citizens and young adults then conducted a telephone census to learn of prospective members for the church. A follow-up mail campaign was conducted among those who indicated potential interest in the church. Mr. Gunther and the members of his census committee then set up a personal calling program for the purpose of visiting those who indicated they would welcome a call. Through this method, First Baptist is able to become acquainted with some of the people who live around its doors and seeks to provide an adequate ministry for their needs.

One problem facing First Baptist Church is its building. Erected for a different day and program, the building is not easily adapted to present-day uses. During the period when there was no pastor, lay people of the church remodeled the kitchen and fellowship hall. This worked wonders in improving the morale of the members and making possible efficient use of the rooms. It is a slow process to remodel a church, but it is thrilling to watch the new life that is coming into First Baptist through its modernization. Outdated programs are being replaced by more adequate ones, and new people are being welcomed into the life of the church.

Constant turnover of membership and consequently of lay leadership are other problems that haunt the church. This is caused both by young persons moving from the community and a lack of vision in seeing clearly how older persons can serve more effectively. The church has to work hard to keep up its total membership from one year to the next. Loss of members through transfer and death without compensatory new membership is a pressing problem. Many of the former members are today in churches started by First Baptist in the nearby Boston suburbs. Some of these churches were assisted through financial loans from First Baptist Church.

A church must serve a definite area now to survive. The days of large membership may be past for First Baptist. However, the lonely and often forgotten persons in the apartment and rooming houses around the church still need and are responding to the church's program for them. Some members feel it may not be many years before a late afternoon worship service on Thursday will be offered to members, visitors, and residents before they leave for the long three-day week end provided by the shortened work week. This service would be in addition to the Sunday morning service, at least for a time.

Mr. Gunther feels there is no simple approach or answer for

First Baptist Church or any other church in the downtown area. He has embarked on a program to make the church's activities meet the always changing needs of the people in the church's community. People who have the privilege of being in churches like First Baptist Church of Boston should rejoice at the exciting opportunities for service that face them in their changing communities.

Central Methodist Church of Detroit is a downtown church that serves almost every age group, but it ministers principally to those sixteen years of age and older. An excellent preaching ministry, supplemented by small discussion groups, brings people not only from the area but also from great distances to this prominent downtown church. A weekday ministry for those in its immediate neighborhood is one of its strong program features.

Timothy Eaton Memorial United Church in Toronto has a Sunday evening worship service that is outstanding among large city churches. Its many through-the-week group activities make it possible to establish contact with many people in the area.

As the needs of the city are endless, so are the varieties of ways in which churches of all denominations are seeking to meet them with Christian programs of concern and commitment. Church extension in the downtown area is not an easy task, for it involves extending the life of the church beyond its present limits. It means taking the church to people who have recently come to the community as well as to the established residents who have not yet been reached.

Many of the estimated forty million people in the United States who have never been inside any house of worship live in the downtown or inner city area. Worship becomes meaningful only as one understands the traditions of the church and the reasons for conducting services according to specific patterns. Therefore, worship training may be necessary in the downtown church as it seeks to reach this group that has not known what it means to worship God.

Training for church membership is considered essential by Christ Presbyterian Church in Burlington, Vt. There prospective members meet in small groups for ten weeks of membership classes. Such training was found necessary before the parish was started in a converted television repair shop in May, 1956. Of the original seventy-three members, only four had had previous Presbyterian affiliation. The original groups were called "Firesides" and were organized on a geographical basis with a cross section of economic and educational levels represented. The small groups of ten to fifteen people enable all to participate as individuals, each contributing from his own unique background to the discussion of questions raised by members of the groups.

The pastor of Christ Church, the Rev. William H. Hollister, has said, "If the church is to meet people today . . . especially people who are molded by our industrial society, it must be gauged initially to their questions and to pointing up the relevance of the gospel to their immediate situation." He feels the small discussion groups are a gratifying church venture, for they are a medium through which real meeting occurs between man and man and man and God.

From the church members themselves has sprung a real sense of the mission of the laity. Members have been active in fighting racial discrimination by helping Negroes—one a doctor, the other a jet pilot—find housing. Looking for a job that would express their conviction that "our parish is judged not on how many people we have or how large a building or budget we can point to, but on how responsible we are to God as His instrument," an adult study group formed a jail committee. When a teen-ager was imprisoned for stealing a car, he found that he had friends in court from Christ Church. They visited him in jail, arranged for someone to give him counsel, and were present during his trial. While he served his ninety-day sentence, the jail committee worked with him and the other prisoners, helping to turn their leisure hours into constructive recreation and rehabilitation.

The members of this mission-aided church have suggested the formation of occupational groups to encourage the consideration of job problems in the light of Christianity. They are eager to be a vital serving and witnessing community in whatever way is needed.

Church extension for a downtown parish involves retooling both program and purpose of the existing church and starting new ministries to the groups of people around its doors. This is a difficult task in which many of today's teen-agers may share, particularly if they join the ranks of the single career group for a time and find their way to a downtown church similar to those described.

THE TRANSITIONAL CHURCH

In this day when the average urban community has a life span of only ten to twenty years without major change, almost every church experiences some transition. A transitional church, sometimes called an inner city church, is one that is located in an area in which the housing is aging and going downhill. The transitional area may actually be only one step removed from a slum. Business and industry may rapidly spread into what was once a residential area, and the social and economic status of the new residents may be lower than that of the previous inhabitants. There is often a mixture of many races in such an area. Almost all ages are present, although the newcomers generally are younger than the long-time residents.

In such an area as this, the church can be considered a bridge. The area is in an in-between time, before it arrives at its next stable state. This period is the gorge over which a bridge must be built. Building this bridge is one important concern of the church in this kind of community.

A transitional church that is truly representative of its neighborhood includes all social, economic, and racial groups of the community and is in truth a link among the different groups present. A transitional community presents a momentous opportunity for the church to act as a means of bringing the different groups together in a Christian fellowship. To accomplish this, the church must build upon the finest of the days gone by and upon the best of the present community, looking forward to a day of service when the area moves into a stable state after the period of transition.

In such a community the doctrine and faith of Christians is brought face to face with the Master's command that we "love one another." Only with love can a bridge of reconciliation be constructed. There is no other timber that can bridge all the fears and misgivings of various people who live in a transitional area. Here, in faith, the church must extend itself into the unknown. No one is ever quite certain how this time of transition will resolve itself.

Here lies one of the greatest fields of evangelism for the church. Children of many ethnic groups may roam the streets in such an area, and the church might open its doors with a day kindergarten and weekday afternoon programs of recreation and craft groups for them. As a congregation attempts to meet the physical and social needs of a person, that person may eventually entrust to the church the far greater matter of his soul's spiritual direction and care.

In the heat of change, the transitional church must temper the reluctance of age to change at all and the impetuosity of youth to change too rapidly before sufficient analysis, thought, and experience have been brought to bear upon a problem. The transitional church must blend these two into harmonious service to the neighborhood, which in turn will look to the church for its spiritual nurture. If the church does not seize its opportunity, the people of the community will turn to secular organizations, even to the local tavern or any other place in which they will find a welcome.

There are many transitional churches that could be cited. One is Mariners' Temple on New York's Lower East Side, which was begun in 1843 as a mission to seamen. Today it seeks to combat narcotics addiction and teen-age gang warfare in a neighborhood in which there are such diverse cultures as Chinese, Puerto Rican, Eastern European, Italian, and Negro American. Through its programs, switch blade knives and bop guns are being put aside and youthful energies are being channeled into wholesome activities.

Two ministers, the Rev. George Younger and the Rev. Rosenwald Robertson, and a children's worker, Margaret Zipse, are welding together, in co-operative enterprises, people who previously would not even have been seen together. Non-Spanish-speaking people are learning to accept and even participate in Spanish-English services. The people are becoming interested and vocal in such civic activities as the Parent-Teacher Association, a health committee that promotes the importance of proper hospital care and antipolio vaccinations, and a neighborhood planning committee that is examining its community needs for a self-renewal program to be conducted by the city. Though God is working through Mariners' Temple to reconcile his children, the battle here, as in other transitional churches, is never entirely won.

Christ Church, Milwaukee, a unit of the United Presbyterian Church in the United States of America, has made a good approach to its declining neighborhood and area. Through the co-operation and assistance of volunteer young people from nearby suburban churches, it has developed an after-school crafts group and a recreational and study program for the youth of the community. The suburban youth groups have also been active as volunteer leaders in the day camping program of Christ Church during the summer months.

The key to programs in this type of church is the eagerness of youth, the calmness of age, and the patience of Job in working in areas that are much in need of Christian help but also are highly suspicious of the church that may have long neglected their needs. People in transitional areas may wonder why the church is trying to help them now. Nevertheless, their suspicion may be worn away through the continued care and concern of Christian people.

THE APARTMENT CHURCH

The apartment house church represents another type of church extension in urban areas. To see the potential in this relatively new kind of church, it should be noted that apartments are no longer limited to the heart of a city. On the fringe of Phoenix, Ariz., apartment houses are being constructed even before individual homes. The Toronto housing authority is erecting apartment units in the suburbs for its citizens who are in some way handicapped, socially, economically, or racially.

In many cities today former mansions and even old apartment houses are being demolished to make way for the great numbers of modern apartments that are springing up. Some apartment developments are home to five thousand or more people.

These new communities that are being created require a new type of church; not one with a new gospel, for that never changes, but one with a different physical structure and a modified program for extending its gospel. Thus the apartment church is emerging. Often such a church is begun by holding meetings in the lobby of one of the apartment buildings. When the group begins to feel that it should be a congregation it may want a more formal church and so remodel two or more apartments into an apartment chapel.

The day may not be too far distant when real estate firms, with a religious concern for tenants, will provide a place in their buildings for a church to be furnished and maintained. Scarcity and high cost of land in the apartment house areas have caused some denominations to consider the apartment church as a practical means of ministering to one growing group of people in large cities.

The apartment church must, as part of its mission, provide a means of fellowship for the people who live in great numbers in the same area but who often do not even know their next door neighbor, much less others in the same building. This may be done through small group discussions, Bible study, and social activities that provide participants with an opportunity to discuss

the issues of the day as well as of their lives, and relate their Christian faith to them. Here the church again can become the institution that binds people of unrelated interests and backgrounds into a fellowship of believers. The church in the apartment can perform a genuine service to the kingdom by uniting some of God's children in worship, study, and concern to be good neighbors.

This church needs to be extremely sensitive to the needs of the apartment dwellers. With the increasing desire to be away on long week ends, many people may be out of the city on Sundays. The apartment church may hold weekly vesper services on Thursday or Friday for those who go away for the week end. Or such groups could meet in the early morning for prayer before going to work. Here in the apartment house is church extension in a new sense. Some of today's teen-agers in time will attend apartment house churches.

THE SUBURBAN CHURCH

Another form of church extension is found on the fringe of the city in the tract home communities that have been mushrooming since 1945. The suburban church's ministry may be to young married couples who are making their first homes in a one- or two-bedroom community, or it may be to older, more prosperous couples who need and can afford to live in the more expensive three- and four-bedroom communities that are conceived and developed on a mass scale.

In the initial stages of development of both these types of suburb, there is the necessity of creating a Christian family from among people whose common denominators may be similar age, economic status, and number of children, but who have little common religious heritage.

Land in the new suburban tract may have been set aside for a church, and the first residents of the area may be entrusted with the responsibility of constructing the first unit of a church during their six- to ten-year stay.

This church is much like a baby in the family. Its buildings may not be complete, but there is the beginning of a church. The finances of the "baby church" are usually extremely strained and limited, much like the finances of a young couple just starting a family. As the "baby church" continues to grow, it stabilizes its finances and builds additional units so that it may more effectively serve its area. More and more families join in this task, and the church, like most of the homes in the first suburban ring, outgrows its physical facilities almost too soon. As it enters into maturity, the church may again increase its program and add another minister to the staff.

But these are the material or physical aspects of the church's new life. The new church must also grow up from childhood to adulthood in a spiritual way. People coming into a new suburban church may be without much practical experience. Suddenly, some of them are asked to serve as deacons, stewards, vestrymen, trustees, church school superintendents, and moderators, and in other lay capacities. The leaders available for such a church generally are untrained for such responsibilities. If they belong to an interdenominational church, they will have little in the way of a common religious experience or training, often coming from many different denominations. One of the challenges they face is to become integrated as the church of Jesus Christ.

Some may come to the church in suburbia asking, "What can we receive from this church?" If they do not receive what they desire, they may shop for another church that more nearly meets their needs. Nevertheless, many remain, and the new church grows and stabilizes itself spiritually. A tradition is built, and small obstacles that upset the church initially are more easily overcome. There may be many lengthy business meetings, and some people may not see eye to eye, but the church and its people grow through such experiences to become mature members of the church of Christ.

A new suburban church may face times of crisis as it finds itself with great numbers of children, a lack of trained teachers, inadequate Christian education facilities, and not enough money to do all the building required—all at the same time. Facing the opportunities created by such crises can be an exciting experience, however, and the way they rise to meet such opportunities sometimes surprises even the members themselves.

What are some of the other difficulties young couples might meet in a suburban church extension situation? They may find that their community has few older couples who possess the wisdom of experience. In a two-bedroom community, there are few people over forty-five and almost all the members of the church live in "mortgage gulch," attempting to buy their home and at the same time financing the building of a new church.

Churches with young families need to provide nursery service in order for parents to attend meetings and services. Some groups may meet in homes and provide a common baby sitter as they have Bible study, prayer, and fellowship. Some suburban churches have more children under twelve than they can handle, and the nursery is one of the most significant phases of the church's life. Some families may even judge the church more on the adequacy of its nursery facilities for their children than on its effectiveness in bringing the gospel into their lives. For many young couples the early years of their marriage revolve around their children. For them the church speaks to their spiritual needs through first meeting the needs of their children.

Young children are frequently sick so their parents are not able to attend church together. The father may stay home to baby-sit while the mother goes with the children who are well. As many of the families have limited resources financially, they often engage in do-it-yourself projects. As a result, some couples may be tempted to attend church only on the first and third Sundays and skip the others to work on their homes. The church may actually have two congregations and seek to unite them into one fellowship. Some of the members who go on the first and third Sundays may remark, "Why, where is everyone?" if they should happen to go on the second Sunday, for instance. The group they normally see on the first and third Sundays might not be present. The church in suburbia needs to recognize and meet this unusual situation.

Many mothers in suburban communities are among those who work outside the home. The suburban church can often profitably provide a day nursery and kindergarten for the children of members and nonmembers who work. This is usually operated on a charge basis and provides a curriculum within a framework of Christian nurture. This service provides a way of reaching many of the couples of the community who would not otherwise have contact with the church.

By meeting one known need the church may demonstrate its interest in the total life of the families in the area. Through its day school program, the church may find additional funds to help finance its Christian education facilities, since these may be used on a six-day-a-week basis instead of only for Sunday church school. The kindergarten and nursery may have a monthly parent-teacher meeting at which parents may learn what their children will be doing in the school during the coming month. This is one way the suburban church may reach out to the new needs that have been brought about by cultural change in this age.

Probably at no time in the history of the Christian church has there been such rapid growth of individual churches in such a short time as in the period since World War II. Every denomination has found it necessary to institute a "crash" program of building new churches. This has been required to provide a minimum of churches for the new communities being built almost overnight.

Many denominations have found that unless a church is started in a community before it is half settled, a new congregation has a difficult time getting underway. This does not mean that the church cannot minister and grow, but it is difficult. Being there when the community is started has proved to be a real advantage, for the church can begin to reach people as they start life in their new community.

In most cases the one or two churches that become the "community churches" and grow much larger in membership, facilities, and program than the other churches in the area usually are the result of wise planning by their denominational

home mission boards. A good site is purchased while the community is being conceived; an initial unit of the church is constructed while the houses are being built; and a minister is called to begin enlisting members for his yet unorganized church while the community is being settled.

Such a church is Village United Presbyterian Church, Prairie Village, Kans., a Greater Kansas City suburb. The community of Prairie Village was planned by a developer, and three-bedroom, expandable homes are the norm. The whole concept of Village Church was that it was to serve the community and its needs with its message and witness. This proved to be the ministry that so effectively enlisted the people of Prairie Village into its membership and expanded its service to the area.

In 1947, the United Presbyterian Board of American Missions realized that in order to begin an effective ministry the denomination needed to provide something immediately for the community. Without waiting for the community to rally around and provide the funds for the first unit of a church and a salary for a minister, the board provided a sum of $100,000 to be invested in an initial three-hundred-seat structure and a home and a salary for a minister.

The United Presbyterian board purchased an excellent site just two blocks from the proposed shopping center and across the street from the site for Prairie School. The church building was constructed at the same time as the new homes. The church got ready in advance for the people. The young minister chosen for Prairie Village was the Rev. Robert H. Meneilly, who had just graduated from seminary. With enthusiasm that often only a young man can have, he began his ministry. Before holding any services, he called on the new residents to let them know of the plans for the church. Although he was only twenty-two years old, Bob Meneilly soon won the hearts and allegiance of the newcomers to the church and its mission.

The young minister realized that the church had to build a community spirit before a church fellowship could be built and maintained. The best way to do this was to provide for some of the community's needs. No church in a new town has the right to assume that it is automatically welcome in a community. The church must win and deserve the respect of the residents by serving their known needs. In this spirit Mr. Meneilly started his ministry. There was no newspaper, so the pastor started a combination church-community paper that eventually had a circulation of 15,000. Later, when no Scoutmaster could be found for the troop and the troop was nearly depleted, Bob Meneilly, although never a member of the Scout movement himself, took on the job and served two years. As the troop grew and became better organized, sponsorship was transferred to the church. Through the community-church paper, the Boy Scout Troop, and the endless hours of calling, community spirit was sparked. Through the church's ministry, people who were strangers began to feel that they belonged together.

The community was composed of people who were newcomers but who had many things in common. They had come to a new home and were eager to become acquainted and have friends in their new community. Being of the same age, they also had somewhat the same income. It was primarily a neighborhood of families with from one to five children, and the church had its future guaranteed in their presence. Naturally, the parents were concerned about their children's education, both secular and religious, and they were looking for a church. The Village Church held the answers to many of the recognized and unrecognized needs of the people of Prairie Village.

The people responded eagerly when the first church school session was held in the church basement in October, 1948. One hundred and fifty pupils appeared, and everyone, from the three-year-olds to the teen-agers, met in one room. The minister used an illustrated sermonet for the lesson. The church school had begun, and the community was excited.

Many residents, having come from other churches and different denominations, looked to the new Village Church for their spiritual guidance and care. In November, 1948, the Village Church sanctuary, which is today its chapel, was ready for use. The first worship service was crowded. The tone of the church's ministry was sounded in Mr. Meneilly's first sermon, "What You Can Expect of Your Church." He told the people that they could expect rebuke where rebuke was needed, revelation from the Word of God, and inspiration.

The church believed that it truly had to know what it meant to be a church before it could welcome persons to become members. The residents of the community had to sense a oneness with one another before they could sincerely become members together in the Village Church. For several months the pastor allowed the congregation to observe what the membership would be like and what the church stood for. Then, in February, 1949, the church was formally constituted, the building was dedicated, and 282 charter members were received.

At first the congregation stressed service to the community, rather than the denomination, and was known simply as "The Village Church." Three-fourths of the members of the new church had not been active in church since their own teens. Whatever their religious backgrounds, the couples had much in common. Most of them were young, had GI mortgages, and had growing families. More and more of them entered wholeheartedly into the church life, serving as officers, singing in the choirs, teaching, or ushering. Later, as traffic jams developed outside the church, men of the congregation took on the task of directing cars between services. The young people of the church developed a bell ringers choir that not only serves the church but also goes out into the community to give concerts upon invitation before various groups.

There has been spiritual growth among the people who make up the congregation of the Village Church each week. Mr. Meneilly sees it in a habit dropped here, and attitude changed there. He summed up his feeling of the ministry of the church in these words: "My conviction is that the church ought to admit everyone, meet each person on his own spiritual level, and bring him to a full personal experience with Christ." After being well underway, the members saw the importance of their wider mission, that of a close denominational relationship, so that today Village Church is part of the United Presbyterian Church. In the congregation's thirteen years of witness, one young man has gone into the ministry and four more are now preparing to become ministers. One is planning for overseas mission work.

Congregations related to almost every major Protestant denomination are now located in Prairie Village, yet the Village United Presbyterian Church still is the only one that counts its members in the thousands rather than in the hundreds. In 1960 its membership was 4,100. On one Sunday the pastor welcomed 136 people to membership; on another, he baptized 38 babies. In 1960 attendance averaged 2,400, and church school attendance was 1,800. With 96 per cent of them pledging, Villagers subscribed to a $350,000 budget in 1960. Since 1947 the congregation had given more than $300,000 to the worldwide mission work of the denomination.

With growing membership has come the need for more space. Building projects have crowded one upon the other. The congregation has built a church and a half-million-dollar education wing that match the facilities of the public schools. After the completion of a large sanctuary in 1957, the church moved briefly to two morning services. Now there are three worship services each Sunday morning to accommodate the large congregation.

Today Prairie Village United Presbyterian Church has a staff of fifteen. Mr. Meneilly, as the senior minister, now spends two-thirds of his time in personal counseling.

In the area of Prairie Village, there are some children who have cerebral palsy and are unable to attend public schools. Village Church has started a cerebral palsy day care center to provide for the needs of these children. During the summer the young people of the church, under professional supervision, also give valuable leadership to this new program.

There is the subtle temptation for such a church to become another club. Instead, it must remain a prophetic witness to the community that needs Christian ideals and moral concepts for life in the twentieth century. People come and go. Mobility among the rising executives in such communities as Prairie Village poses leadership problems for the church, although the over-all turnover in Village Church is only about 12 per cent of the membership in a year. This type of church in three- and four-bedroom home developments is more stable than the two-bedroom community, for it has older people to help with church leadership.

In such a community as Prairie Village, young people have a growing responsibility. Many of them begin their mature church experience in similar circumstances, and the training they receive will be reflected in the type of membership and leadership they will give in the churches to which they will move as they live in new communities still to be built throughout the nation.

With large numbers of World War II babies now reaching adulthood, there will be a great spurt in building new communities and churches in the next five to ten years in Canada and the United States. Like their parents, these young people of today will be faced with the problems of selecting an appropriate site for a church, choosing a minister, and surveying a community to learn its needs and to plan how the church can meet them. Soon these will be opportunities they will face as they move to two-bedroom and even three- and four-bedroom homes.

The Village Church, large, growing, and extending its ministry to fields of changing needs, can be duplicated by churches in many cities in Canada and the United States. The churches are under different names, but their tasks and their sense of urgency are similar. The Panorama Baptist Church near Los Angeles is like the Village Church, but it has added a significant ministry through its six-grade day school in which a full-fledged religious and well-rounded secular educational program is provided. St. Leonard's Anglican Church in Toronto provides a strong preaching and counseling ministry for its community.

In the growing suburban three- and four-bedroom developments, young people, through their vital youth programs, are making their contributions to the total life of the church by being volunteer workers in day camps for inner city children, by serving in choirs, by serving as junior board members and assistants in church school classes, and in many other ways.

THE CHURCH IN THE CUSTOM-BUILT SUBURBS

On the average, one young person out of every twenty in youth groups across the country finds himself in the suburban church that is set in communities of three- and four-bedroom, custom built houses. In such a community, the congregation and the building may be new or the congregation of this suburban church may be the continuation of one formerly located in an inner city area. As the neighborhood of its original site changed, and as most of its members moved out to the custom-built suburb, the membership felt the church should follow its congregation rather than change its ministry to meet the needs of the people around its doors. Some might label this church a "class church," because its community and members economically and socially would generally fall into the upper middle class and lower upper class groups.

Such a church may have a difficult role to play. There may be the tendency for it to conform to the concepts, desires, and customs of the members instead of being a transforming fellowship. The church may have to cope with the problem of not becoming a spiritual country club for the residents of the area. This type of church should not lack leadership or finances, but it may lack dedication and commitment on the part of its members.

This type of church may not feel the need to extend itself to the dispossessed and less fortunate in its community, for there are few if any such persons. Such a church, however, has many opportunities to lend financial assistance and leadership to inner city, downtown, transitional, and even other suburban churches. Because it has ten talents, much is expected of this type of church. It may have difficulty in measuring up to the demands and requirements set for it in these demanding days. Those who live in such a community and are members of such a church have a great opportunity for witness through service to the total city area in which it is located.

Actually, only a minority of present-day youth are part of such a church, but those who are should recognize the great challenge such a church has for service and leadership.

THE RURAL-URBAN FRINGE CHURCH

In the rural-urban fringe areas, the city and the country meet. Conflicting ideas, cultures, concepts, and needs may meet head on as the old is confronted by the new. Such conflicts of interest pose an exciting challenge for the church.

Many churches in the rural-urban fringe may be over fifty years old. Their buildings may be small and centered primarily around the sanctuary with limited Christian education facilities. There may be a tendency for the established leaders in such a community to hold to the old manner of doing things and to reject newcomers' suggestions and ideas, whether or not they are sound. Such a situation does not create an inviting atmosphere in which to find a new church home, yet it is increasingly the product of the population explosion and the expansion of the urban areas of our nations. Careful leadership is important in such a situation. The church and the community needs to be prepared for the expansion of the city into the outlying rural areas, for many languishing rural churches may find new life as a result of this expansion.

The rural-urban fringe church is very much a part of the scene across the nation. In Canada, Thornhill United Church, which is in a small community outside Toronto, is a representative example. Here is a church that for years served in a quiet village, close but unrelated to Toronto. A rural ministry was more than adequate. Then residents of Toronto became interested in the country and began to move out to the Thornhill area. Thornhill United Church has adjusted well to the conflicting interests of the old-timers and the newcomers, and a program is underway to help meet the needs of the new resident.

Pittsford United Church, near Rochester, N. Y., is a similar church. Situated for years in a primarily farming and dairying community, it now must adjust its ministry to the growing numbers of business executives from nearby Rochester who are moving into its area. The Pittsford United Church, like those of other denominations, is erecting new buildings to meet the growing needs in an area that is taking on new life.

THE VILLAGE CHURCH

Out beyond the metropolitan areas, in the thousands of small towns and villages throughout Canada and the United States, stand thousands of small village churches. Often white and weather beaten, they still are beacons of the gospel of Jesus Christ. Some denominations still have the majority of their churches in villages and towns of less than ten thousand population, but most of their members attend churches in urban areas. Among them are the United Church of Canada, The Methodist Church, the Congregational Christian Churches, and the American Baptist Convention.

Many villages and their churches are also facing changes.

As farmers in Canada and the United States are able to produce more and more food with the aid of fewer people, the former agricultural emphasis of the majority of these villages and towns is changing. Some are dying; others are finding new life as industry begins to decentralize and move to small communities where there may be a ready labor market and there is room for physical expansion.

The churches in such communities may not have grown for years and actually may have been declining for some time. Declining membership has caused many village churches in the past ten years to close their doors. Others have merged with churches of the same or different denominations; still others have federated with one or more churches to form a single church to serve the community. The village church still has a significant ministry to render.

Often the village church requires much care, and even a new addition may be necessary in this day when small classes in separate rooms are needed for adequate Christian education. Fully trained and ordained leadership is often difficult to obtain and hold because of the shortage of ministers. The low salaries that many of the small churches are able to pay often make it impossible for one church to support a full-time minister alone. Thus several churches link themselves together in a larger parish or circuit, which may be served by one or more pastors.

There are many opportunities in the village church. One great asset is the close fellowship that exists in a small community in which people understand what it truly means to be members one of another in both joys and sorrows. This fellowship usually can be a real help to the church. In the small village church, through the dedication of its church school teachers, many of the pupils receive Christian training that equals the finest of educational programs in larger urban churches.

In this type of church, the need for the co-operation and assistance of young people is vital. They may serve as teachers, ushers, and sometimes they may have positions on the official boards of the church.

CHURCHES FOR MILITARY COMMUNITIES

Since the founding of the United States of America, the Christian church has followed its service personnel wherever they went. The prevailing Cold War, threatening the world since the end of World War II and the Korean conflict, has made it necessary for free nations to maintain their military might. Today 2,500,000 men and women are in the United States peace-time military forces. The chaplaincy corps of the various services seek to be the church away from home for the military personnel in the field and on the base.

Situated at the permanent military bases, the armed forces chapels are used by chaplains of the Jewish, Catholic, and Protes-

tant faiths. The altar area in each chapel can be quickly changed to display the religious symbols traditional to the group worshiping in the chapel.

Chaplains are commissioned officers in the Army, Navy, Air Force, and Marine Corps. In addition to counseling the men and women in their charge, they conduct church services for members of their particular faith, and some hold classes in religious education. Unlike most clergymen, chaplains have in their congregations a preponderance of men, everywhere, that is, except at bases where women are being trained.

The armed forces chaplain faces many opportunities to be a vital link between the serviceman and the home church, for the armed forces chapel is only representative of the local church or synagogue. The chapel is not an entity unto itself, so that when a person joins the church while in the services, he is urged to affiliate with a church back home or one in the civilian community near the base.

One area in which the chaplain especially needs the assistance of the home church is in maintaining a link between it and the serviceman. If they do not hear from their own church, many young men and women in the service feel that their church back home has lost interest in them. One authority estimates that this situation is aggravated by the fact that three out of every four letters sent by chaplains to their servicemen's home churches go unanswered by the local pastor.

In the armed forces chapels, as well as in the churches in communities near military installations, the faith of service men and women may either be fostered and developed, or, if left unnurtured, may wither and die. All too often a person who does not have a well-grounded faith will, during his military duty, lose even the little bit he may have had.

Rootlessness, lack of inhibiting home and family pressures, and a social whirl identified with military functions all contribute to keeping some service personnel away from the church. Another factor that plagues congregations either in the armed forces chapels or in the civilian community near a base is the high mobility of servicemen brought about by frequent transfers and discharges. A service family may stay in a community or on a base for only a few months. Some people feel that the leadership potential of service personnel is rarely given an opportunity to reach its peak, and consequently the chapel or church suffers. The United Presbyterian Church, however, believes that despite high mobility armed forces personnel who are trained for such responsibilities as elders, church school teachers, or youth leaders are able to give valuable service, even though they may not stay in one church for very long.

Today a good many men in the armed forces are married and prefer to live off base with their families whenever possible. Local churches in communities near military installations have a particularly important ministry to perform if armed forces families are to feel welcome and at home in the area. Armed forces families sometimes slip in and out of town without the local church being aware of their presence, and those living off base frequently are not effectively reached by either the base chaplain or a local minister.

In order to help the service family fit into the pattern of the local church, some denominations have established special programs for areas in which there are many service families.

The United Presbyterian Church conducts this phase of its ministry to military personnel through parish visitors, one of whom is Mrs. Clarence B. Davenport. Her territory is Mount Holly, N. J., and the trailer camps, towns, and developments that surround it. The people she seeks to bring into a happy relationship with the community and the church are servicemen stationed at Fort Dix, Maguire Air Force Base, and a Nike missile site, and their families. Her headquarters is at the First Presbyterian Church of Mount Holly. There she works closely with the local pastor as well as with the chaplains who minister to those men and their families who live on or near the three military posts.

As soon as Mrs. Davenport hears of the arrival of a serviceman and his family in the Mount Holly area, she pays a personal call at their home. If she learns that they are Presbyterian, or if their denomination does not have a church in the area, she invites them to attend the services and programs of the Mount Holly Presbyterian church. Back in her office she passes on the names of the newcomers to the pastor and to members of appropriate organizations within the church, such as the service-wives callers.

A veritable information bureau, Mrs. Davenport has been asked by new residents in Mount Holly to recommend baby sitters, pediatricians, practical nurses, or household help. Foreign-born wives, living in and around the area, are of particular interest to Mrs. Davenport. She has helped to set up, with other organizations, classes in English and citizenship, and she has aided them through periods of loneliness and homesickness by introducing them to other residents from their own countries. She also introduces American newcomers to older residents with like interest.

The Mount Holly Presbyterian church is known to people thereabouts as a church that is available to help them solve their problems. These include marital infidelity, that is sometimes the result of long separations brought about by husbands' overseas duty; tensions created by childrearing; and social misunderstandings that sometimes arise in interracial marriages.

When the wife of an Army sergeant serving in Korea came down with phlebitis, Mrs. Davenport stepped in and took care of the house and the children while the wife was at home. After the wife went into the hospital, the parish worker found a temporary home for the children, cleaned up the apartment, regularly visited the patient, paid the hospital bill from personal funds, and drove the wife home in the Davenport station wagon. Mrs. Davenport also wrote regularly to the husband in Korea, assuring him that his wife and family were being cared for by the church.

In addition to Mrs. Davenport's work in Mount Holly, the United Presbyterian Church is conducting similar ministries in Altus and Lawton, Okla.; Anchorage and Fairbanks, Alaska; Annapolis, Md.; Bellevue, Neb.; El Paso and San Antonio, Texas; Lompoc, Monterey, Oceanside, Sacramento, and Vacaville, Calif.; Forrestal Village and Rantoul, Ill.; Newport, R. I.; Peru, Ind.; Grandview and Warrensburg, Mo.; Tacoma, Wash.; and Washington, D. C. Other denominations are finding different ways to minister to armed forces personnel, but their concern is the same—that the gospel be offered to all in an effective way.

THE COLLEGE OR UNIVERSITY CHURCH

The college or university church was not a common phenomenon before 1900. It has come into its own since World War II, with the great influx of college and university students all across Canada and the United States.

This type of church differs from most other churches in three ways. First, it is usually located near an educational institution and serves as the church home for students who belong to its particular denomination. Second, this church often conducts special student work and sometimes maintains a student house on campus. Third, the college church has a fluctuating congregation, 50 per cent of which may be students.

The greatest need in such churches is a strong witness to the academic community, both to students and to faculty members. While at college, many students rethink their childhood faith. Unless an effective campus ministry is offered, many find their previous faith inadequate and turn away from the church. On the other hand, these persons who will be assuming positions of leadership and influence in national and international life in the future can have their faith built up during college years and can learn to apply that faith to life's changing needs in a realistic way.

The university church also must have a dedicated core of people from the local community to keep it strong during student vacations and provide the continuing leadership needed by such a transient community.

The college or university church will be a growing and crucial ministry in the future as the number of people attending institutions of higher learning increase in the next decade.

THE TRAILER CHAPEL

The trailer chapel is becoming increasingly a way of extending the church to the changing needs of some of the people. In some instances it must become the focal point in the lives of those whose diverse backgrounds, employment, education, and families provide no other unifying symbol or force. The only other common ground such people may have is the fact that they all live in mobile homes.

At first the church may move into a trailer community with its own mobile unit that is specially constructed for church use. Later, in the center of the trailer village or park, a permanent structure may be built. People who live in trailers are growing in number and their mobility demands the stability of a strong religious faith and church to assist them in becoming a part of something meaningful.

One example of this type of church extension, sponsored by the Board of National Missions of the United Presbyterian Church, is the trailer ministry, conducted by the Rev. and Mrs. W. Theodore Allison, west of Grants, N. M. In this rapidly expanding area there are four uranium processing plants nearby and a number of trailer courts. The Allisons are established in one of the largest courts and carry on their work both from their own large trailer home and in Westminster Chapel, a specially equipped trailer unit.

A significant ministry to many of the residents of the trailer courts all about the city of Detroit has been carried on for more than twenty years by the Rev. Mary Murray. In her ministry she has worn out three trailers and also has established a permanent chapel. The mobile chapel that Miss Murray takes from trailer court to trailer court is a welcome sight and brings a ministry to both adults and children in often forgotten areas of the city. Miss Murray's work is supported by the American Baptist Home Mission Societies, and the Detroit Association of American Baptist Churches.

The apartment church, the armed forces chapel, the university church, and the trailer chapel are all products of the new age and culture of this century. Young people can give creative leadership in seeing that churches recognize the growing number of people needing such types of churches.

OTHER FACETS OF CHURCH EXTENSION

Specialized ministries, for example, to the deaf and to the foreign born, are being carried on by individual churches in some large cities both in the United States and Canada. The First Deaf Baptist Church of Los Angeles has a congregation that is composed of people who come long distances for worship, Christian education, and fellowship conducted in sign language. Some churches have special earphones installed in the pews for those who are hard of hearing.

With the great influx of non-English-speaking refugees into Canada and the large numbers of Spanish-speaking peoples in various large cities in the United States, language churches again are taking on importance. In the United States the churches that have large Spanish-speaking congregations usually have services in both English and Spanish. In Canada some churches have three and even four distinct congregations, each speaking a different language. English classes and foreign language services are held for these people both on Sunday and during the week. The eventual goal of the foreign language churches is to have services only in English, but this is achieved only when everyone feels enough at home in the language to worship in it.

A variety of essential church extension ministries are carried on in sparsely populated areas of North America. In Canada these include: a mobile ministry to the trailer camps at lumbering and mining sites, a chaplain's service to train-based frontier work gangs, the United Church of Canada's Sunday School of the Air that provides lesson materials to remote families, the student caravans that go out to remote areas during the summer, and drive-in church services for summer weekenders.

In North Dakota there is a converted street bus that serves as a mobile chapel or wayside church. Operated by the Archdeacon of the Missionary District of North Dakota of the Protestant Episcopal Church, the bus travels between twelve and fifteen thousand miles a year. The Ven. Thomas McEligott stops from one to four days in each place, holding services of Holy Communion and Morning and Evening Prayer. Sometimes he

conducts services in homes of parishioners, at other times he officiates before the altar of the Church of the Good Shepherd, which is the name of the mobile chapel. Archdeacon McEligott is able to visit some places only once a year. He goes to others as often as once in two or three months.

Through this ministry the Episcopalians of the remote areas of North Dakota are held together as a Christian family who know that they are not forgotten by their church.

Throughout the continent the churches are reaching into the lives of both children and older persons through their nationwide health and welfare agencies.

Although denominations still maintain some institutional care for normal children who may come from homes broken by divorce, desertion, or death, the trend today is to place such children in foster homes and limit institutional care to those who require special treatment facilities because they are mentally retarded, emotionally disturbed, or physically handicapped. The atmosphere of a natural family unit is considered so important today that some denominations, among them many branches of the Lutheran Church, provide statewide case work services to children in their own homes. While there are some eight hundred Protestant child welfare service agencies in the United States, there are only four hundred Protestant institutional homes, which is a good indication of the trend away from institutionalism.

Care of the older person, sixty-five years and older, is becoming an increasingly important consideration both in the United States and Canada. There were 17 million people sixty-five and older in the United States in 1960, but their number is expected to jump to 25 million by 1980, according to the Federal Council on Aging. Today 6 per cent of the United States population of older persons live in institutions, and there is a long waiting list for acceptance into residential homes for the aging and nursing homes for the chronically ill.

Most people prefer to continue living in their own house or apartment after they retire, but the infirmities of advancing years sometimes make it necessary for them to have outside assistance of some kind. Aware of this need, some denominations include in their programs for senior citizens not only residential or institutional care, but also such home services as shopping, financial and family counseling, recreational activities, housekeeping aid, and transportation pools. Some of the church agencies find foster homes for their older people, and a number of denominations have established retirement communities in which senior citizens live independently in small apartments but enjoy the benefits of community health and recreational facilities.

YOUTH'S RESPONSIBILITY

On youth's shoulders will be the responsibility for church extension in the future. All the churches have a peculiar and special ministry to perform right where they are. Youth can assist the church in extending itself to the needs of young people their own age who are not now being reached. Many young people will remain unreached through every service of worship, every class of the church school, every gathering of the youth group, unless Christian young people help to extend the church by reaching out personally and bringing all within the compass of the church into the knowledge of Jesus Christ.

V

YOUTH'S TASK IN EXTENDING THE CHURCH

New ventures tested and proved successful
by other youth groups may guide you as you, too,
strive to extend the church. Your opportunity
is now, for the future won't wait.

HAROLD P. DE ROO, DIRECTOR,
DEPARTMENT OF YOUNG PEOPLE'S WORK,
REFORMED CHURCH IN AMERICA

O magnify the Lord with me,
and let us exalt his name together!

PSALM 34:3

V

YOUTH'S TASK IN EXTENDING THE CHURCH

MAKE A PROFILE OF YOUR COMMUNITY
ANALYZE YOUR CHURCH
WHAT ABOUT YOUR YOUTH GROUP?
REPORT ON YOUR STUDY
YOUR ROLE IN THE FUTURE
THE INFLUENCE OF YOUTH

CHAPTER V
Youth's Task in Extending the Church

Today's young people in their teens know more about the world, its people, and the universe in which they live than young people have known at any other time in history. Yet with all the knowledge of the twentieth century, man still has not mastered the way to live in peace and harmony with his brothers. The way of the Master himself still holds the only solution, "love your neighbor as yourself." To the church of Jesus Christ, which they inherit from those who have gone before them, young people must contribute fresh ideas for new ways of extending the gospel to those who have not been reached.

Many of the answers to the opportunities and the solutions to the problems of this day lie within the hands of young people. How will they help to meet the demands that have come upon them so swiftly that, almost before they are aware of the dawning, they find themselves in noonday brightness? How will youth meet the demanding cry for that which speaks to the wants of the rootless, the insecure, and the lonely?

Young people today live in a time in which adventure is sacrificed for security. This is an age in which the uncertain is pushed aside for the certain and acceptable. But, in this age of conformity, the youth of today who are the adults of tomorrow must, nevertheless, discover new and different ways of meeting the old, old needs of mankind.

The answer to the ancient problem of how best to live in the world is not to be found in dealing only with the great crises of the world, but rather by starting right at home in one's own family, church, community, village, town, or city. One must face squarely such personal questions as the best kind of family life possible in this age when people spend less time than ever before either at home or on the job. One must look closely at his own church and community to see how they can meet more effectively the needs that surround them.

Perhaps descriptions of the various types of churches and communities have stirred you to ask questions about your own. Maybe you are wondering how much of this is true of your home, you church, your community. How should you approach your own situation so as to speak more dynamically to the needs of the children, youth, and adults in your church and community? What can be the future of your community? What stage of transition is it in? How can you find out?

These are valid questions, and there are ways to find the answers to them. How may you know what to do for your community and church unless you know what their needs are and the ways in which the church is currently seeking to meet them? A study of your church and community, therefore, should be considered.

MAKE A PROFILE OF YOUR COMMUNITY

Begin by first considering the community in which your church is located. Use as your guide the descriptions of various types of communities given in Chapter III.

Is your community inner city, transitional, or suburban? If suburban, is it a one- or two-bedroom community, a three- or four-bedroom community, or is it in the rural-urban fringe?

If out in the open country, is it a small village or a town?

What are the characteristics of your neighborhood? It is strictly residential? Does it have many shops, a school, a theater, or maybe a factory or two? Is there a large park or a highway running through it? List its characteristics.

With this brief but important knowledge of your neighborhood, consider the type of church yours is.

Is it an inner city church, a transitional church, one in a suburb composed primarily of young married couples with small children, one in a suburb with older couples and teen-agers, one in a custom-built community, or one in the rural-urban fringe?

Is yours a village church in one of the many small towns in Canada or the United States?

Is yours one of the less well-known churches such as an apartment house church, a trailer chapel, a university church, or an armed forces chapel?

After noting both its community and characteristics, take time to write a description of your church. Then list what you believe it is doing to minister to the people of its area. If you are not familiar with all phases of your church's ministry, check the weekly bulletin, if there is one, or ask one of the key lay leaders or the pastor or director of Christian education.

In order to determine the adequacy of a program, you must know whom the church is trying to reach. It is of vital importance to know what groups and ages are present in your area in order to plan a program adequate to meet their specific needs. To determine the proportion of the various age groups in your community, you should make a profile of your area, showing the number of people in each age group. You can base your profile on the information that you are able to obtain from your national census bureau.

In the United States general population characteristics, such as age and sex, and in some instances detailed characteristics, such as economic or social status and types and condition of housing, according to states, may be secured through your local Department of Commerce field office or from the Bureau of the Census, Washington 25, D. C. Before ordering, check to learn what is available for your particular city, town, or area.

In Canada the reports of the 1956 census include population distribution by sex and age. Here again check with the Dominion Bureau of Statistics in Ottawa before ordering so that you will know which reports will best suit your particular needs.

To give you an idea of how a community might look if its inhabitants were categorized as to age and sex, three charts of United States communities are shown. The first is for a transitional area, the second for a stable area, the third for a new suburban community. These figures are based on the 1950 census.

You will see that the chart of the transitional area shows that there are large numbers of children under the age of nine and of adults over the age of sixty-five. Children from ten to fourteen and from fifteen to nineteen form the smallest groups. Their families have left the community and they have been replaced by families with children under the age of nine. The age groups twenty to twenty-four, twenty-five to twenty-nine, and thirty to thirty-four, are about equal in number. They represent the newcomers to the neighborhood who bring with them children under the age of nine. The percentage of males and females is almost identical in such a neighborhood.

The significant differences in age-sex groupings between a transitional and a downtown church are interesting:

First, children under the age of nine are generally fewer in the downtown area than in the transitional area. Likewise, the number who are in the age groups ten to fourteen and fifteen to nineteen are smaller in proportion to the total.

Second, there is a significant number of persons between twenty and thirty-nine, many of whom are single young adults. In the transitional community, families are the main grouping.

Third, the number of persons between forty and forty-nine is considerably less than the number of young adults.

Fourth, those over the age of sixty-five usually represent the largest number in the downtown community.

Fifth, women considerably outnumber men, probably 55

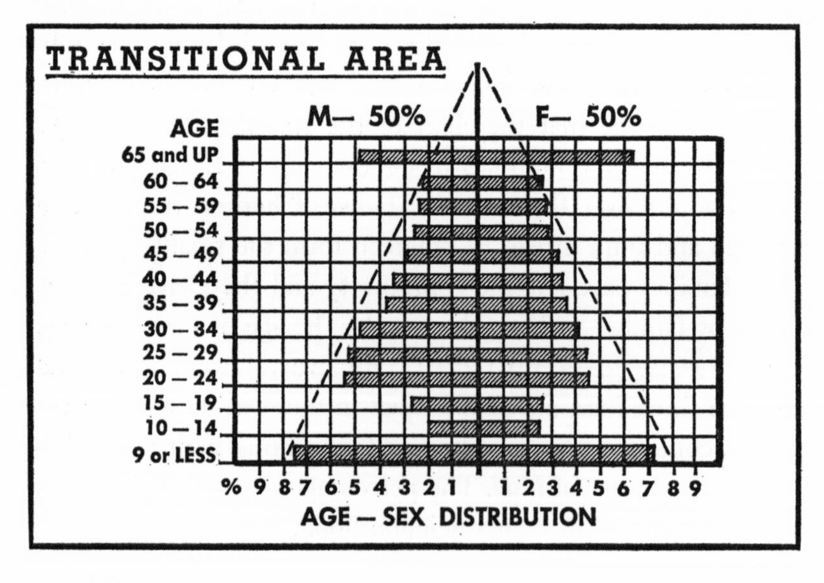

per cent to 45 per cent in most downtown areas, although in some instances the reverse is true.

Does this grouping of ages best describe your church's community? If so, does your church take such facts into account in its planning?

The chart of a stable residential area may illustrate the situation prevailing in many communities. If yours is a suburban community that has been settled for some twenty to fifty years, the age groups present in your neighborhood would be much like those shown in this chart. Likewise, many small villages will also have such age distribution. This chart would not be representative of a new community, nor of the downtown or transitional area. The main characteristics of a stable residential community are that it is an aging neighborhood with a large number

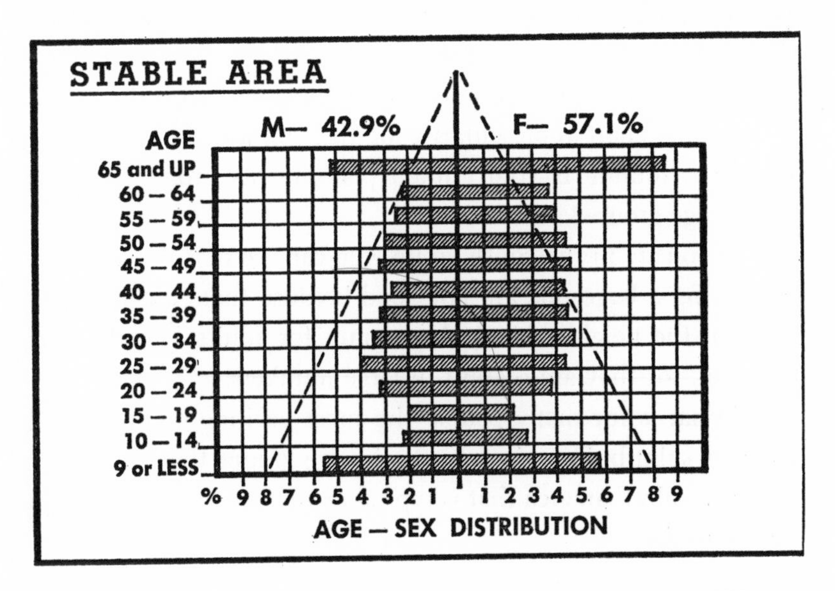

of persons over forty-five. However, senior citizens are not as numerous here as they are in the downtown area.

Parents in this stable community are older on the average than those in the transitional area, yet there is only a small number of children ranging in age from ten to nineteen. There sometimes is a sizeable number of children under the age of nine.

In this older and more stable neighborhood, there is a fairly equal distribution of men and women in the age groups between twenty-five and fifty-four. This is especially true in small towns. The number of people twenty to twenty-four years old is small, because young men and women in this age group either are away at college or have left home as young married people or as single career men and women. Note also the fact that, in this old stable community, women outnumber men, 57 per cent to about 43 per cent. Approximately six out of every ten people are females. This is because women outlive men, and they often continue to live in such stable communities after their husbands die.

Is this chart representative of the community where your church is found? Is your church planning its program for the proper age groups?

If you are in the youth group, you can see that the prospects for having a large one are not good because there are few teen-agers in the neighborhood. A program for adults is mandatory, however, for they are present in large numbers.

What is for many people the most exciting community is the new suburb. Examine closely the age groups that are present in a new suburban area that is typical of the one- or two-bedroom communities.

Characteristic of the new suburb is the fact that 25 per cent of the population is under nine and only 6 per cent is between fifteen and twenty-four. The number of young couples, especially those between twenty-five and thirty-four, is large.

The difference between the age groups present in the new suburban area and the suburb with three- or four-bedroom homes is that the number of children ten to nineteen is much larger in the latter than in the former. In the more expensive neighborhood, there are also more adults in the age range of thirty to forty-four and perhaps a few more persons over the age of fifty. This latter group, however, comprises a small percentage of the community's total population.

The custom-built home community, or third suburban area, is primarily made up of those who are over the age of forty-five

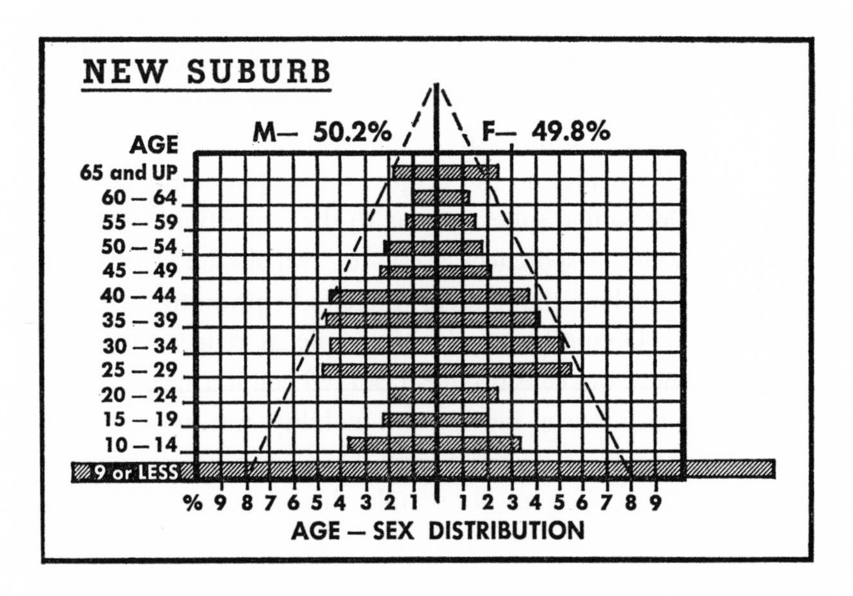

and in the teens from fourteen through nineteen. There are few from twenty through twenty-nine.

Once you have determined the ages represented in your community, you next need to consider some of the other characteristics of your area. First secure a map of your area on which streets are clearly marked. If your church has more than five hundred members, you will probably need a map of the entire city or town. Next note where the business district is and mark it in color on the map. Then ask the following questions about your area:

Is the neighborhood growing? If so, how rapidly?

Is it an area in which most homes are alike?

What racial groups live in the area and where? How rapidly are the various racial groups increasing and in which direction are they moving? Plot their movement.

What is the average income of the people? What do they do for a living? What occupations predominate in the neighborhood? Are there more professional people than semiskilled laborers living in your area?

How frequently do the people in the community move?

In order to find some answers to these questions, you probably will want to spotcheck a one- or two-block radius around your church, asking the residents there to help you to the best of their ability. Do not be surprised if people are reluctant to reveal their income. Your census bureau can tell you if a special survey, covering such items as income and mobility, was made for your neighborhood. If so, secure a copy. Do they move more or less frequently, according to your sample, than the average American who moves once in every five years?

ANALYZE YOUR CHURCH

Now that you have considered the type of neighborhood you live in, who your neighbors are, and perhaps what their economic status is, you are ready to reconsider the church's present ministry.

Begin by examining closely the church you attend. Does it seek to enlist all people from the neighborhood in its services and activities?

In order to become a growing and effective church, the average congregation should receive the majority of its new members from the residents living around its doors. What about your church? Where do your members live?

Some authorities may differ in techniques for making a survey of a church's community and its membership, but for the purpose of this study the following method is suggested:

On the map of your area mark in red the exact location of your church. Then, with a compass set to the same scale as the map, draw a circle of a one-mile radius with your church as the central point. Continue in this manner to draw two- and three-mile circles. When this is completed mount the map on cardboard, either permanently by using wallpaper paste or temporarily with thumbtacks.

Next obtain from your church office a list of names and addresses of the people who have joined the church within the last four years. Have the church clerk or pastor indicate whether these members are now active or inactive in the church and which of them have accepted leadership responsibilities. Use a blue pencil to make a dot on the map indicating where each active member lives. Use a green pencil to make a dot on the map indicating where each inactive member lives. Use a star to indicate each active person who is a leader.

When you have finished, count the number of blue and green dots falling within each of the circles and beyond the circles and then total the number of active and inactive members. If more than 50 per cent of the members who joined within the past four years came from a two-mile area around the church, your church may be considered to be doing a basically effective job of evangelizing the neighborhood. If yours is a new suburban community, more than 60 per cent of the new members should come from the two-mile area around the church. If less than half the persons who joined your church within the past four years come from this two-mile radius, then leaders and youth of the church need to ask themselves why they have not been more effective in reaching the people around their doors.

Is the church friendly? Visit another church some Sunday and note how many people, if any, greet you as a stranger.

In your church are strangers made to feel at home and welcome or are they ignored?

Do strangers receive the kind of welcome you personally would want to receive if you were a stranger? If not, what steps can young people take to improve the situation? Next Sunday morning, immediately following the close of the service, see if you can pick out the strangers. Those who know one another will probably turn to friends and begin talking, but the strangers will stand alone for that fraction of a minute and then move quickly to the door and leave.

Are members cared for after they are welcomed into the church? How?

Whether people are building a new church in the suburbs or extending a church into new fields in the inner city or small village, the ability to reach and hold new members depends on the effectiveness with which new members are assimilated into the church. Face-to-face discussion and social groups often are required to assist new members in becoming an integral part of the church fellowship and in strengthening their personal Christian witness.

Are new members given positions of leadership and responsibility in the church? If less than 10 per cent of the church's leaders are among those brought into membership within the last four years, your church may not be effectively using the talents of its new members.

On the average, one out of every five new members received into a Protestant church today becomes inactive within one year. What about your church?

How many of the new members you located on the map are already inactive? Why not ask a few of them why they first became united with the church and why they are now inactive?

It has been found there are few inactive members among those who have been given leadership roles to fill and those whose close friends are also members of the congregation, according to several studies recently conducted.

WHAT ABOUT YOUR YOUTH GROUP?

Probably the organization within the church in which you can be most effective in extending the church is the youth group.

Do you actually know why it exists and what its goals are? How are they achieved?

When were the last new members of your group received?

Have new members come primarily from the families who are also members of the church?

Where do the members of your youth group live?

On the same map on which you plotted the residences of the new members of your church, mark where the members of your youth group live. You might use a double circle to indicate the teen-agers.

Do the majority of the members come from the two-mile area around the church? If not, can you give any reasons why you are not reaching the young people near the church? Have you honestly tried?

In your study you should next list what you do for the church in assisting it to serve its community. Then try to think of additional ways you can assist the church in extending its ministry. Maybe your group could profit by knowing what some other groups throughout the country have done.

In one church there was a large number of elderly members who could not attend services regularly. The youth group secured a tape recorder and each Sunday taped the congregational worship service. During the following week they took the recorder to the homes of the shut-ins. This was done on a scheduled basis and gave the elderly people an opportunity to worship with the congregation in this manner.

In Florida, where many persons vacation and many retired people settle, a youth group co-operated with the church members in setting up and operating a "church taxi service" to bring to the church school and worship services those who had no means of transportation. The church's telephone number was included in a weekly advertisement in the local newspaper. The people were asked to call the church number between 9 A.M. and 10:15 A.M. on Sunday, and the young people manned the office and dispatched the cars to pick up those desiring a ride. This has increased the attendance significantly and has made the youth group one of the most active organizations within the church.

In another church the young people believed that the chapel should be open for meditation and prayer every day of the week, not just on Sundays. They found there were a number of people in the congregation who thought that it would be helpful for despondent people and others if they could hear a Scripture reading, a prayer, or a hymn during the time of their special need.

The youth group took this as a project. They secured a used juke box and, with the guidance of their youth adviser and their pastor, made recordings of hymns and prayers, passages of Scripture, and short meditations on selected subjects. These were catalogued and placed in the machine. Now a person going to the chapel can select a record that may be helpful to him in time of need. This service has tripled the use of the chapel. The young people have made it their responsibility to see that new recordings are made and that the record player is kept in good working order.

In one large city a group of teen-agers overheard a young person on the bus say, "Wouldn't it be nice if there were a number in the phone book that people could call if they were lonely and wanted someone to talk to for a minute." The young people discussed the idea at the next meeting of their youth group. Now they list in the yellow pages of the telephone book this notice: "Lonely?—Call CI 5-2098. We'll be happy to talk with you." When a person calls that number, he hears a recorded voice express appreciation that he has called. He is then asked to leave his telephone number and first name. The recorded reply offers words of encouragement and asks the caller to be at his number in an hour to receive a return telephone call. Assigned young people check periodically to see if anyone has called in and left a number. If so, they call the number and talk with the lonely person.

Through this service, a number of people who were at their wits' end have found new meaning and encouragement for living. Others have been helped through a blue mood. A number of people have come into their first meaningful contact with the church by this method and are now active participants in the church.

Perhaps your group could do something of this nature or maybe provide a dial-a-message service that would give a one-minute message and a prayer.

A youth group in Washington state, assumed responsibility

for making a personal telephone call to each member who missed more than two Sundays of worship. In their call they expressed the church's concern that the member had been absent and inquired whether anyone were ill or if there were any way the church could give assistance. This helped the church and the pastor in several ways. If there were reasons why the pastor should call, such as illness or personal trouble, these were discovered early and referred to the minister. This approach has in large measure been responsibile for less than 5 per cent inactivity on the part of the total resident membership.

The youth group of a large downtown church in Chicago delivers the bulletins of the Sunday services to many of the nearby hotels. This worthwhile activity, carried out on Saturdays, has helped travelers, tourists, and others, to become aware of the church.

In a small village church, one youth group set up a round robin correspondence with the young men and women who had gone into the armed forces. They did not restrict the letters to their church alone but included men and women from the entire community. This meant that many who otherwise might have been forgotten, except by their own family, felt really missed and appreciated. The concern and efforts of this youth group helped to extend the ties of the home church and neighborhood to the persons who were on duty in the armed services.

In another village church, a youth group was particularly interested in photography. On the adviser's suggestion they decided to prepare a photographic history of their community. They went from house to house, stopping to photograph it and the occupants and to find out when the house was built and by whom, where the present occupants came from, and what they did for a living. They assembled a slide sequence with a script that they recorded on a tape recorder, so the presentation would run smoothly and could have a musical background to make it more interesting. One evening, after the church's annual ice cream social, they presented their story, "Your Neighbors and Your Community."

This may sound simple enough, but it had far-reaching results. The community, which had many people who were at odds with one another, began to undergo a change. There developed a greater unity and interest in the community's welfare and in the very people with whom they had differed before. Sparked by this effort, there developed in community and church a spirit of co-operation and mutual concern.

These are but a few ways in which youth groups have sought to extend the church to meet more adequately the needs of the members and of other people around its doors.

REPORT ON YOUR STUDY

You have compiled information about the community around your church, looked at where the church's new members have come from, and examined the program and membership of your own youth group. Now you need to assemble all these data and then take positive steps.

Study the information you have collected and any you may have obtained from local city planning officials, then try to predict the future by asking yourselves some questions:

What is the future of the community around the church? Will it continue to grow, according to the judgment of city officials? If so, how much? What will be the population peak, and when will it be reached?

What zoning changes are anticipated in the church's area? Are any urban renewal projects scheduled for the neighborhood?

If there is to be an urban renewal project, how will it affect the people living in the area now? What type of housing or office buildings will be constructed?

Are any new highways to be located near the church? If so, how many church members will be displaced by such construction?

In a Montana village a six-lane expressway went through the community. Its construction not only caused destruction of the homes, it also required the remodeling of the local church. Even small towns are subject to rapid change in these times.

What racial groups are expected to live in the community within the next five to ten years?

How old is the housing in your neighborhood?

After you have answers to some or all of the above questions, seek to determine what they mean for the church.

Will the church grow or decrease in membership?

Will its program need to be changed to meet the new situations that are to come? If so, how can youth help make the program more adequate for the new requirements?

If the church has not been gaining 50 per cent of its members from the area within a two-mile radius of the church, what programs of enlisting new members should the church begin?

If the church also loses to inactivity one out of five new members within the first year of their membership, what can be done to prevent this?

If the community around the church contains racial groups that are not in the church, in what ways can young people assist to make them welcome?

If the church is not as friendly as might be desired, in what ways can youth help?

Would it be a good project for your group to assist in greeting people, especially young people, who enter and leave the sanctuary each Sunday?

Some churches register each person present on Sunday. Could it be a project for your group to check the registry and make a list of the new young people present so that they may be called upon during the week?

From the map, you know from what areas your youth group gains new members. What methods could you employ to enlist more young people? Consider also why a new person might want to participate in your youth program.

Why did you become involved in the group?

Are there activities and a friendly spirit that make it attractive to others?

Is the group a "wanting" or a "giving" group as far as the total church is concerned?

Are you satisfied with what the group is doing to reach others?

After you have the answers to such questions, draw up some long-range recommendations that you feel would help your church and youth group to be more effective in ministering to its members and the neighborhood. When your recommendations are completed, be sure that your group makes a report to the responsible church leaders.

YOUR ROLE IN THE FUTURE

As young people help the church to serve effectively, they prepare themselves for the time when, with others, they will build new churches in the suburbs, apartment churches in the inner city, mobile trailer churches in the mobile villages. Tomorrow, today's youth will help to change the downtown church's program to meet new needs and help the village church to see its new opportunities for Christian service.

In the future there will be scientific advances beyond anything previous generations have known. Advances in the spiritual realm will depend largely upon the Christian leadership you and others of your generation will give. How many new churches will you build in your lifetime? How many persons will you lead to a deeper understanding of their faith? How many communities will your church serve effectively? How concerned spiritually are you for tomorrow's world? Only you have the answers.

Emphasis so far has been on what young people can do together to assist the churches to extend their work to meet new needs. But what about you individually? What will be your personal role in the future?

The late teen years and early twenties are the time when many young people begin seriously to make vocational choices. If an individual agrees that God is his Father, then certainly he has a responsibility to seek God's will for his life before making a vocational decision. It is very important that every Christian give a thoughtful answer to the questions, "What does God want me to do with my life? To what is God calling me?" Is it his will that you should be in one of the church-related vocations? If the answer to this last question is yes, preparation will doubtless involve both undergraduate and postgraduate study. If, on the other hand, the answer to that question is no, you should determine that whatever you do you will do as a dedicated member of the Christian laity.

THE INFLUENCE OF YOUTH

It was said of two of Jesus' young followers during the first century of the Christian era, "these men . . . have turned the world upside down." In this day that is also being said of youth around the world.

In 1956 the free world was thrilled and saddened by the gallant but bloody days of the Hungarian uprising in which freedom-loving youth and adults fought side by side against the armored tanks and other modern weapons of the Soviet occupation forces. In a military and political sense, they did not win; but in a moral sense the people of Hungary did win. They proved to the world that there still beats within the hearts of enslaved people the will to be free, even against overwhelming odds. Of those Hungarians it can be said that they almost turned the world upside down.

In 1960 it was the youth of Japan who, through their uprisings and demonstrations, brought about the cancellation of the visit of the President of the United States to their country. In Turkey, Korea, Africa, and Latin America, young people have shown so strongly their passion for causes in which they believe that they have, in some instances, been willing to risk even their lives for them.

For the majority of American and Canadian youth, there seem to be few burning issues that excite their imaginations and

stir up their energies. In too many instances, they seem to be content to express themselves in hot rod races, panty raids, football rallies, or beatnik demonstrations of protest. Fortunately a dedicated group of American youth revealed positive Christian protest in the sit-in strikes that began in Greensboro, N. C., early in 1960 and spread to other southern cities. In the sit-ins Negro youth, along with some white sympathizers, fought peacefully against the discriminatory practice of not serving Negroes at certain lunch counters. An offshoot of the sit-ins were the kneel-ins in which Negro and white youth attempted to break down racial barriers in houses of worship by entering and praying in churches normally closed to Negro worshipers.

Such demonstrations are encouraging signs of youth's concern for justice and the kind of constructive action in which American youth can give Christian witness. If this is to be, in the truest sense of the term, "the age of youth," then every young Christian must be God's instrument through his own individual witness in all phases of his life. If Christian youth does not act while there is still time, all will be lost—for the future won't wait.

NOTES

[1] From a speech, "The Last Farthing," by the Rev. Edwin T. Dahlberg to the American Baptist Convention, Rochester, June, 1960.

[2] "A Rise Is Reported in Unwed Mothers," *The New York Times*, May 29, 1959, p. 7.

[3] Figures in this paragraph are based on surveys conducted by various denominations and especially Church Strategy Studies, Division of Church Missions, American Baptist Home Mission Societies, New York, 1956-1960.

[4] *The Canadian Council of Churches News Bulletin*, December, 1960, p. 2. Used by permission.

[5] *The Crack in the Picture Window*, by John C. Keats. Boston: Houghton Mifflin Co., 1957, inside front cover. Used by permission.

SET IN ELECTRA 11 POINT LEADED 4 POINTS
MANUFACTURED BY SOWERS PRINTING COMPANY, LEBANON, PA.
JACKETS AND PAPER COVERS BY AFFILIATED LITHOGRAPHERS, INC., NEW YORK, N. Y.
PAPER: S. D. WARREN'S OLDE STYLE WOVE
TYPOGRAPHIC DESIGN BY WARREN JOHNSON
BINDING BY LOUISE E. JEFFERSON